THE WHOLE SELF LIFESTYLE FOR WORKING PARENTS

A PRACTICAL 4-STEP FRAMEWORK TO
DEFEAT BURNOUT AND ESCAPE SURVIVAL
MODE FOR GOOD

SARAH ARGENAL, MA, CPC

For permission requests or for reprints or excerpts, contact the publisher at hello@argenalinstitute.com or at www.argenalinstitute.com. Our books may be purchased in bulk for promotional, educational, or business use.

ISBN: 978-1-7351254-1-1 (eBook)

ISBN: 978-1-7351254-0-4 (Paperback)

Library of Congress Control Number: 2020909767

Cover design by Ronald Cruz at www.cruzialdesigns.com.

First Edition: June 2020

Published by The Argenal Institute LLC.

Printed in the United States of America

The Argenal Institute LLC

539 W Commerce St #2091

Dallas, TX 75208

www.argenalinstitute.com

To Joey, Beckett and Weston...
You make every moment precious.

CONTENTS

1

NOT ANOTHER PARENTING
ADVICE BOOK

There's no shortage of how-to information for working parents these days. Expert advice is everywhere: Google and Amazon search results, our social media feeds, podcasts, parenting groups, or our parents and siblings and friends. We're inundated with advice and opinions. Self-help is a $11 billion industry full of experts (and not-so-expert novices) who claim they can help you fix all of your problems, usually quickly and easily:

- How to manage your time to make room for what you love.
- How to streamline your morning routine to avoid chaos.
- How to plan a week's worth of meals over the weekend.
- How to discipline your kids when they misbehave.
- How to stay connected with your partner despite

sleepless nights, financial stress, and unreliable babysitters.

This is potentially all helpful advice, *if* it happens to work for you. But what about when it *doesn't* work for you? What if you've followed all of these instructions religiously, and you still haven't found relief? What if you've checked off all the boxes that are supposed to lead to happiness, and you still find yourself drowning under the weight of endless obligations, expectations, and responsibilities?

In that case, you may feel like a failure because the clear-cut instruction manuals aren't working for you. You may be thinking: *What's wrong with me? This seems to work for everyone else. I must be doing something wrong. I just need to try a little harder to make it work.*

Nope. You're not the problem.

The advice you receive as a busy working parent in modern society will sometimes be a good fit for you; other times, it won't. It's that simple. That's not a character flaw, it's just a fact.

There are a lot of things in life that are conducive to how-to instructions. Navigating the pitfalls and challenges of modern working parenthood isn't one of them. Working parenthood is complex. It's an "inside job," as the saying goes. It's impossible to design a parenting advice book that will be a perfect fit for *your* unique personality, needs, strengths, and goals in this particular season of your life. There are too many variables to consider. It's impossible for anyone else to tell you what to do or how to do it with any reliability. As much as we want one, there will never be a "one-size fits all" solution for working parenthood.

———

THIS ISN'T A PARENTING ADVICE BOOK

You won't find hot tips or life hacks or shortcuts for happiness in this book. You won't find my Top 10 Rules for Working Parents, or a list of "secret" tactics to make your life easier. I'm not going to tell you what to do, or how you should live your life. I don't presume to know what your unique combination of challenges are, much less how to fix them. That's for *you* to figure out. Instead, I am here to guide you along that (often baffling) path of self-discovery.

This book will offer you a roadmap to build your *own* personal instruction manual for *your* unique experience as a working parent. As you work your way through this book, you'll pinpoint the hidden, underlying source of *your* specific struggles. You'll identify your deepest desires and your long-term goals. You'll clarify your individual needs and strengths. You'll get a birds-eye view of the different areas of your life. After you have that big picture perspective of what you're dealing with, then you can dive deep into the areas that require your time and attention in *this* moment.

This book will help you clarify *your* answers, rather than encourage you to implement anyone else's, including mine. This book explores what can happen when you release the fear and commit to doing the hard work of *understanding yourself.* Once you know yourself on a deeper level, you'll learn how to craft a life that finally fits who *you* are, right now. You'll learn how to stop settling for that toxic cycle of burnout that most modern working parents find themselves trapped in. When you apply the principles outlined in this book, you'll embrace the *real* adventure of working parent-hood and all of the treasured moments that await you.

Everything is either an opportunity to grow or an obstacle to keep you from growing. You get to choose. Wayne Dyer

WHO AM I TO WRITE THIS BOOK?

This book is what I call a "functional memoir." I share my own experience as a burned-out working mom, since the most natural way we learn as humans is through story. But I also outline the four practical steps I took (and continue to take) to transform my experience from one of burnout and frustration to one of adventure, joy, and connection. I integrate my diverse professional training, personal experience, and the research I've accumulated to approach working parenthood from a holistic point of view. This is my story, but it's supported by twenty years of work with parents from all walks of life.

As a child of divorce, I was raised in two blended families in two very different environments. I spent most of my childhood in a small hippie town of Mt. Shasta in northern California, but spent summers and holidays in the heart of the conservative Midwestern suburbs of Cincinnati. These were two very different realities. I learned how to adapt to different circumstances early in life.

As a homeschooled student from 10-15 years old, I traveled up and down the California coast on a sailboat with my family. I spent most mornings finishing my schoolwork so I could spend the rest of the day snowboarding at our local ski park in the Winter or swimming at the lake in the Summer.

As a young college student from 15-19 years old, I was self-motivated and focused on my studies. I graduated from the University of California at Davis when I was 19 years old with a degree in political science. Six months later, I received my Paralegal Certificate from the University of San Diego, then immediately started my first job as a litigation paralegal at a law firm in downtown San Francisco.

As the youngest person in just about any situation, I felt a lot of pressure to succeed. Most people assumed I would fail, so I had to work overtime to prove them wrong. It was years before I recognized that external pressure as a natural source of my perfectionism. Type-A behavior led to an unwillingness to give up in the face of adversity. Those traits helped me succeed in many ways, but they also became severe obstacles to happiness later in my life.

Seeing the reality of life in Big Law up close, I realized fairly quickly I no longer wanted to pursue my childhood dream of becoming a lawyer. Following my first real bout of burnout, I took a sabbatical and went backpacking around Thailand on my own for a month. When I returned, I started a psychotherapy graduate program at the University of San Francisco. Over the next two years, I worked full-time at the law firm during the day while working toward my master's degree at night. Two years after I got my M.A. in counseling psychology with an emphasis in marriage and family therapy and adult development, I obtained my Professional Coach Certification. A few years after that, I became a certified court mediator. I specialized in helping people with three specific struggles: strengthening their most important relationships, creating a healthy life balance, and navigating major life transitions.

Over the last 25 years, I have applied my education and experience in a range of different professional environments. I spent the early years of my career as a litigation paralegal at some of the world's largest law firms in San Francisco, Silicon Valley, San Diego, and Boston. My specialty areas included complex corporate litigation, patent infringement litigation, intellectual property, and employment law. In 2012, I shifted my focus to become a litigation support analyst where I integrated my technology, project management, and legal experience to consult with litigators about the best way to analyze and present their electronic evidence in preparation for and at trial.

As part of my psychotherapy training, I worked with dual- and triple-diagnosis clients in a residential substance abuse recovery facility in San Francisco. All of my clients were battling life-long addictions, as well as mental health disorders, and some also had terminal physical illnesses.

As a certified court mediator, I blended my marriage and family therapy experience with my coaching and law experience to support couples who were struggling in their marriage and considering separation. Together we found common ground they could build on to strengthen their marriage before it devolved into divorce.

As a professional coach, I helped high school students who were transitioning out of the grip of addiction and into college to develop critical life skills, such as decision-making, impulse-control, organization, and community contributions. I also coached new college graduates who struggled to clarify their identity and purpose after college. I helped them navigate the transition out of college and into the real world as they established key relationship skills such as healthy communication, assertiveness training, and conflict resolution.

I also taught psychology, communications, and strategies for success classes as an adjunct instructor at Everest College in Salt Lake City, Utah. I balanced that out, just for fun, with teaching snowboarding at Park City Mountain Resort in Park City, Utah.

I've traveled around the world to Thailand, South Korea,

Costa Rica, Mexico, France, and England. Most of the time, I was alone and forced to rely on my instincts, common sense, and the generosity of strangers to handle new and challenging situations. The adventures I've faced on my travels have formed a sense of independence and a deep respect for other cultures that I carry with me to this day.

I've learned from a lifetime of love, loss, and failure, as we all inevitably do. Throughout it all, I've been a dedicated student of philosophy, meditation, and metaphysics. I was exposed to the catholic traditions throughout childhood, but have integrated elements of Taoism, Stoicism and Buddhism into my beliefs and daily practices. My spirituality is a personal compilation of what makes the most sense to me. It is the foundation of my life, my source of meaning, guidance, and soul growth.

I became a mother for the first time in 2013. Today I have two healthy and wonderful little boys who teach me more about my true purpose than anyone ever could. They are my ultimate guides as to what matters most in life. I find surprising lessons in every day with them.

Today I blend all of these experiences in my work at The Argenal Institute, a company I founded in 2015 to explore the complexities of life for modern working parents. Our primary goal is to discover what makes working parenthood *work,* and work *well,* for some families and not for others. I take a holistic approach to help working parents overcome burnout *for good,* so they can finally create lives they love. I work with individuals and groups, which gives me an inside look at the range of struggles working parents face in all different aspects of their lives. I also host the Working Parent Resource Podcast, where I have in-depth conversations with experts to understand the full scope of this burnout epidemic that's crushing working parents today.

I've had a full life. Many say I've had a "different" life. I don't put much stock in that. Everyone's life is unique. But I have found that my unconventional experience, both personally and professionally, often leads to a different perspective. I find I make unexpected connections and sometimes recognize patterns others aren't paying attention to. I want to share some of those insights with you.

A NOTE ABOUT CONTEXT

My privileged experience is one of an educated, middle class white woman in America. That's the perspective I bring to this topic. I'm ambitious, educated, and career-driven, but I also strive to stay grounded and live a meaningful life. I'm a recovering perfectionist, but that also often translates into being self-reliant, analytical, detail-oriented, and resourceful. I spent two decades establishing myself in my career before I became a mother. I have financial security, a loving marriage, a supportive network of extended family and friends, good health, and a variety of other advantages that so many parents don't have.

I share my background and experience to provide context. I think acknowledging context in the realm of personal growth and problem solving is critical. In our burdensome information age, it's an element that's easily overlooked. Many of us are so desperate for answers that we search frantically for a one-size-fits-all instruction manual. We think if we can just do what our friends or colleagues or our favorite role models do, our lives will end up looking just like theirs. It's a tempting myth, but it's a myth, nonetheless. I'll share the process that has improved my life as a working mother, but it would be disingenuous for me to share my story without acknowledging the many advantages that I take for granted.

That said, I have worked with thousands of people in a variety of settings over the last twenty years as well. The approach outlined in this book has been used to support parents from a wide range of demographic, socioeconomic, ethnic, and educational backgrounds. This approach is also based in decades of research and psychological theory. It's an entirely customizable framework, so the principles I share can be applied to your situation regardless of the circumstances of your life.

You'll also notice that I tend to use traditional cisgender-specific terms and titles to ease the text flow. I recognize that not everyone will fall into the gender profiles, family structures, or other categories as I outline them. I encourage you to disregard any titles or pronouns that don't fit for you, and update the questions raised throughout this book to best reflect *your* identity.

This Book is for Working Moms

This book was written for ambitious moms who spent a decade or two establishing themselves in their career just to find their lives turned upside down when they started their family. It's for women who don't want to, or don't have the option to, stay home full-time with their kids. It's for moms who want to continue to grow and thrive in their professional life while also being an involved and engaged parent.

This book is for women who are accustomed to pursuing and regularly exceeding their goals, mastering skills, and receiving all of the accolades of an overachiever. It's for those working moms who are struggling to apply the skills that made them successful in the workplace to their reality at home.

To those working moms, this book will help you integrate *all* aspects of your personality, including some of the "soft skills" that aren't always valued in the traditional male-dominated workplace, such as flexibility, patience, humility, and empathy. You'll develop a whole new list of tools for your working mother toolbox. And you'll learn which tools work best in different circumstances in your own life.

This Book is for Working Dads

I've spoken with countless working dads who are struggling with many of the same work-life conflict issues busy working moms are. But society doesn't offer a model for how modern dads can blend the various areas of their lives, either.

Many dads are navigating this experience of working parenthood from a different perspective than moms. They apply different skills and have developed different approaches to fatherhood than earlier generations. What I talk about in this book is from my perspective as a working mom. But to the extent you are a working dad struggling with similar challenges of blending work, family, and life, I want this book to be a resource and a guide for you as well. We have minimized the dad's role in the family for generations, and it's time to evolve.

We need to give working dads access to the tools they need to be involved and engaged as fathers, just as we encourage moms to step up in leadership roles and thrive in their careers. We're integrating new realities for *both* moms and dads, and it requires support on both sides.

This Book is for Working Parents Who Are Struggling With Too Many Demands

I was drawn to specialize in the mental and emotional well-being of working parents for one overwhelming reason: their lives are about as complicated as it gets. I see people of all stripes struggling with burnout in this world. I figured if I can help committed working parents create a meaningful and fulfilling lifestyle, then others could apply similar strategies with success.

Our families are all different. Whether you're married, divorced, single, widowed, gay, straight, transgender, non-binary, gender nonconforming, and any other combination of identity profiles, you may be feeling lost in your experience of working parenthood. This book will help you find your *own* answers, whatever the makeup of your family or the circumstances of your life. Here are some universal characteristics that unite all working parents who will benefit from this book, though:

- You work in a professional setting, either a corporate office environment, a home-office, or you've started your own business. You may work part-time or full-time. Whatever the setup, you're invested in your career.
- You're very established in what you do. You love your job (most days) and get a lot of personal fulfillment from your work. Your career was your primary focus and a fundamental part of your identity before having kids.
- You're financially stable, but you're also motivated to continue working in part to maintain your current lifestyle. This lifestyle

often makes you feel "trapped," like there's no way to escape the hamster wheel.

- You're in the habit of striving to meet other people's agendas, goals, and expectations. You're motivated by external rewards such as praise, accolades, promotions, awards, or money. You've lost touch with your sense of *intrinsic* motivation, and as a result you're often controlled by outside influences.

- You're in a "hyper-speed" routine. You're afraid if you slow down, you'll lose momentum and everything you've achieved so far.

- You're also very tired from having to switch gears from all of the different roles you play in your life right now. The context switching is driving you crazy. There's a lack of congruency of self across facets of your identity and your life as a whole.

- You realize you're missing essential parts of your kids' childhood. You're missing the little moments, like putting your kid to sleep or listening to a story from school because you're too distracted with work, and it's killing you. You want to be present in your career, but you also long to focus on your kids. You feel like you're failing at both jobs and don't see a way out.

- Your identity, and your role in your family and your relationships, has shifted considerably since having kids. But you're so exhausted and distracted with what's "urgent" that you haven't had a chance to re-calibrate your sense of who you are. That internal confusion is causing anxiety, feelings of depression, and shame as you navigate your journey as a parent.

- You used to get a lot of confidence from your career. But now you're falling short of expectations due to increased responsibilities at home. You feel anxious about the trajectory of your career now that you're a parent. You're stressed out because you know you're capable of more, and you know your boss and co-workers and clients know you're capable of more as well. But you just don't have time to deliver and focus the way you used to. You spend your day-to-day life managing one "emergency" after another. You can't catch up and are terrified it'll all come crashing down any minute.

- You love your partner, but there's too much conflict, distance, and disconnection in your relationship these days. You aren't sure how to reconnect with each other. You've become roommates, household managers, and co-parents. The focus on your marriage gets pushed aside for other commitments.

- You feel a persistent low level of depression because you're trying to fit too much into a single day, but none of it is very meaningful to you. The people and activities that *are* meaningful to you are put on the back burner until you can "make time" for it... which never happens. Life feels like a nonstop grind.

- Your sense of overwhelm prevents you from implementing extensive changes in your life. You're spinning too many plates, and you're afraid you'll drop one (or all) of them if you make too many changes in your life all at once. So you try to apply "quick fixes" to the different problems in your life, which either don't work at all or don't last long-term. You naturally revert into old, unhealthy patterns as soon as you get stressed or busy again. You're starting to realize these small changes aren't enough to alleviate the overwhelm and exhaustion you feel in every area of your life. You need a holistic shift in your life but are too tired and afraid to pursue it for real.

- You wonder how you'll make it through the next couple of decades like this. You know something has to change, but you have no idea where to start. So you put your head down and work harder and faster. But it's not helping. In fact, it seems to be making things worse.

This Book is for Working Parents Who Want to *Enjoy* Their Lives

Regardless of the structure and status of your life, this book is for anyone who wants to enjoy this *one and only* life they have to live. This book is for parents who are searching for a full and meaningful life. This book was written for working parents who have a *different* kind of life in mind than the one perpetuated in modern society.

- You want to be in control of your own life. You want to reclaim your time, energy, and focus so you can prioritize the things that matter most to you.
- You want to enjoy more time with your kids,

partner, friends, extended family, and have more time for yourself - without the guilt!

- You want to feel confident and successful in all of your various roles. You no longer want to feel like success in one area of your life comes at the expense of another area of your life.
- You want a secure and connected bond with your kids, regardless of how many hours you see them. You want the time you spend with them to be filled with love, respect, and joy.
- You want a loving and playful marriage that's built on trust, communication, and shared values.
- You want to have positive and harmonious exchanges with your family. You're ready to let go of the stress that often intrudes on the morning and evening routine in most working family households.
- You want to feel like you're succeeding in your career and able to pursue your passions while still staying engaged in and managing the other aspects of your home and family.
- You want to feel like you have a whole, complete life that's aligned with your deepest core values. You want the different areas of your life to stop feeling so segmented and fractured and in competition with each other. You want integration and congruency across the various parts of your life. You want what you do in one area of your life to *support* fulfillment in the others rather than detract from it.
- You want to focus mindfully on your personal growth. You want to continue becoming a better

version of yourself. You want to have time to relax, reflect, and re-charge.

- You want to feel confident about how you respond to the unpredictable situations that inevitably arise throughout parenthood. You want to trust in your ability to respond with intention.
- You want to be mentally, physically, and emotionally healthy and self-confident. You want to view life challenges as the vehicle to opening up and refining different parts of who you are.

This Book is for *You*

We're capable of so much more - within ourselves, in our families, our careers, our companies, and our communities. We have the information, technology, and the freedom to make meaningful shifts in this new era of parenting and work. It's time to apply what we know to create a healthier and happier culture, both at work and home.

This change doesn't happen on a surface level, though. The process of creating a life worth living can be hard and uncomfortable and messy. It can take a long time. It usually includes some uncertainty and pain. It often consists of repetition of life lessons before they "stick." That is why a lot of people, especially working parents who are already overwhelmed, avoid this process. They choose to stay numb to their lives and inadvertently get trapped in a cycle of struggle instead.

The very nature of self-development, of discovering who you are *now* so you can make intentional choices about your life, is the key to finding success, happiness, and growth. It doesn't have to be an intimidating and aversive process. It can be rewarding and deeply meaningful, even if it's accompanied by tears and pain at times. Making lasting changes in life isn't always glamorous, but it's worth the effort.

So many people want to bypass this hard work. They're paying the price by experiencing a "lite" version of their lives. They're hurtling toward a life of regrets, not to mention physical illness, mental health issues, conflict, and suffering along the way.

In this book, I will help you defeat burnout in this demanding and unpredictable world so you can finally start *enjoying* your life as a working parent. All you need to do for now is make a conscious choice to reject the survival mode trap. Once you do that, this book will offer a sustainable and straightforward framework to construct your *own* unique path as a working parent.

A PARENT IS BORN

Looking back, I had a very two-dimensional view of parenthood before I had kids. I knew becoming a mom would change my life. I understood on a surface level the logistical changes I would go through. I could never have predicted the level of self-discovery, personal growth, and commitment it would take to *enjoy* the journey of parenthood, though. Now I have greater respect for the full-life transformation that takes place when a *parent* is born.

The life of a parent, and the life of a *working parent* specifically, is not for the faint of heart. It's a non-stop obstacle course for your soul. Over time, I've learned that this transformational process, while terrifying at times, can also be a lot of fun. Even when I stumble and skin my knee, it draws my attention to wounds that are ready to be healed.

We're going to bypass the surface-level advice in this book. There's plenty of that out there already. We're going to go deeper. We're going to get more personal. We'll explore the transition one experiences on a *molecular* level as they transform from an ambitious professional into a self-confident *working parent*: someone who juggles passion, love, commitment, and perseverance in every area of life without sacrificing one thing over another.

This book holds an invitation to begin living your life from the *inside out*. It encourages you to take actions that will lead to real results, genuine connections, and deep contentment. This book is about living your best life, no matter what that life looks like. I'm not promising it will always be easy. But if you're deliberate, you'll build momentum and the process will become more intuitive over time.

WHAT YOU CAN EXPECT FROM THIS BOOK

This book has three distinct parts:

Part 1

In the first part of this book, we're going to get very clear about what's causing the burnout epidemic among working parents in modern society. Burnout is occurring everywhere around the world, for a variety of different populations. We'll drill down into the complex combination of reasons why working parents in particular are struggling. You'll get a clearer picture of the full scope of the challenges you face, so you know what you're *really* dealing with here. Many of these variables may be concealed as we deal with the fallout from coronavirus but make no mistake: they remain hidden in the shadows and will resurge if we don't address them. I'll also share a bit of my own transition from a burned out and unhappy mom to someone who's created a fulfilling life. You'll get a general feel for what this transformation looks like over time.

Part 2

In the second part of this book, we shift the focus to *you*. I translate everything we talk about in the first part into a proactive and action-oriented process you can integrate into your own life. My signature process, the Whole SELF Lifestyle™, is a modern approach toward working parenthood that helps working parents address the logistical and psychological challenges they face as they try to blend work, family, and life in modern society. I'll walk you through my 4-step framework, the Whole SELF Lifestyle, so you can create a *personalized* roadmap to understand and improve the essential areas of *your* life. You'll identify the underlying source of your problems, and then customize solutions to those problems that fit who *you* are today. Once you have that in-depth understanding of yourself and your situation, you can make more effective choices based on what you really need. This part of the book contains exercises, questions, self-reflection prompts, action steps, and resources to help you improve your life as a working parent. You'll also discover the best people and tools you can turn to when you need support, encouragement, and guidance.

Part 3

In the final part of this book, we'll talk about how you can escape survival mode *for good*. You'll learn how to integrate the principles of the Whole SELF Lifestyle into your daily life on a short- and long-term basis. You'll discover the best circumstances under which the Whole SELF Lifestyle framework can be applied, and how you can maintain progress over time.

RECOMMENDED RESOURCES

Included at the end of this book is a list of suggested reading materials, podcasts, and links to research and resources that are mentioned throughout this book. A list of these materials is also available in the Bonus Library for ongoing reference.

BONUS LIBRARY

I'll be integrating free bonus materials throughout this book, which you are invited to download for free from our **Bonus Library**. These resources will help you go even deeper on your path toward self-discovery. You can access everything in the Bonus Library by going to www.wholeselflifestyle.com/ working-parents/bonus-library.

WHOLE SELF LIFESTYLE™ COMPANION WORKBOOK

This book is interactive and designed to help you find your own answers. You're welcome to answer the questions as they appear in this book. If you're someone who does well with journals or workbooks and would like to work through the exercises in this book on paper, I've created **The Whole SELF Lifestyle™ Companion Workbook** as an additional tool for you. This physical workbook is available at: www.wholeselflifestyle.com/working-parents/companion-workbook.

2

MY "I CAN'T DO THIS ANYMORE" WORKING MOM MOMENT

It was just an ordinary February afternoon in the suburbs of San Francisco. The weather was a comfortable and sunny 70 degrees. My husband, Joey, and I were out at lunch, one of our first dates since our son, Beckett, was born six months earlier. It was a beautiful afternoon and we were having a great time. I certainly didn't expect my life to change course as dramatically as it did that day.

Joey and I were deep in the fog of new parenthood. I had just returned to my job as a litigation support analyst at a law firm in San Francisco two months earlier, during the Christmas holidays. It wasn't a bad time to go back to work after a generous five-month maternity leave. Most people were on vacation, so the pace of the office was slow. I got to ease back into the relentless routine of sleepless nights with the baby, a grueling and unpredictable train commute, and around-the-clock demands from frantic attorneys. As a family, we were adjusting to our new reality of diaper bags and daycare drop-offs and pickups. Joey and I were slowly coming to terms with our new identity as working parents.

As soon as the new year arrived, my co-workers became antsy to have a break after covering for me while I was "on vacation," as they called it. Work heated up fast as we headed into January. My schedule went into overdrive.

Here's what a typical day looked like for us in those early months, once we were really into the swing of things:

- **5:00 a.m.:** Beckett wakes up for the day. He is definitely not going back to sleep. I bring him into our bed to nurse him and snuggle before we all have to face the day.
- **5:30 a.m.:** I hand Beckett over to Joey and hop in the shower. Joey gets Beckett dressed and ready for daycare.
- **5:45 a.m.:** Add last-minute bottles and other accouterments to the diaper bag for Beckett's 12-hour day at daycare.
- **6:15 a.m.:** Joey and Beckett head out the door (Joey and I split drop-off and pick-up duties). I have 30 minutes of peace to apply my makeup, style my hair, and get dressed. As soon as I look presentable, I grab my purse and coffee tumbler and race to the train station.
- **7:00 a.m.:** I snag one of the last seats on the train. I catch up on work emails and mentally plan my morning while I sip coffee. Sometimes I sneak in a podcast or article too.
- **8:00 a.m.:** Once I'm in my office, I hit the ground running with a list of matters that need my immediate attention.
- **12:00 - 1:00 p.m.** (*whenever I can sneak it in*):

I hide in the lactation room with my laptop. I simultaneously eat lunch, pump milk for my little guy, and work.

- **4:15 p.m.:** Glance at the clock and realize I have five minutes to catch the next train home. I grab my expressed milk, laptop and purse, and sprint down the street to the train station. On the days I make it in time, I grab a seat and keep working. On the days I miss the train, I have to wait another 20 minutes for the next one, knowing I'll have to stand for the hour-long train ride home and will inevitably arrive after my son's daycare center closes.

- **6:00 p.m.:** Pick up my little guy from daycare. It feels like he's grown three inches since I saw him that morning (I actively suppress the mom guilt). He falls asleep in the car on the way home, sabotaging my plans for a smooth bedtime routine.

- **6:30 p.m.:** Drop everything in the kitchen so I can finally nurse my beautiful and snuggly son. I relish 20 minutes of calm, reveling in his sweet baby breath and soft fingers.

- **7:00 p.m.:** Bath time. Lotion. PJs. Read. Snuggle. Nurse one more time and get in as many kisses as I can. Wave hello to that stranger I used to recognize as my husband when he gets home (a.k.a. Dad).

- **7:30 p.m.:** Put my son in his crib, drowsy but awake, just like all the books recommend. I cross my fingers that tonight will be the night he thinks to himself, *"Okay, I see what they're doing here. I'll*

SARAH ARGENAL, MA, CPC

just snuggle with my favorite lovey and hit the hay. Got it!" No such luck.

- **7:45 p.m.:** Curl up on my bed with my timer, counting down the seconds until I can rescue my little guy who is screaming bloody murder. I imagine he's thinking: *"What the hell?! I haven't seen you ALL DAY, and now you're abandoning me in this room. What are you thinking? Get in here and pick me up, pronto!"*

- **8:00 p.m.:** Give up on sleep training for the night. Nurse my baby to settle him down. Watch his cries subside and breathing quiet. Stroke his soft cheek. Take in his already-getting-too-big body. Plead for time to slow down.

- **8:15 p.m.:** Carefully (*carefully...* it's like defusing a bomb) transfer my (finally) sleeping baby boy into his crib. Head downstairs to help Joey, who's working on dinner for us.

- **8:30 p.m.:** Switch on Netflix, inhale some dinner (*when* did I eat last??), and finish the project I abandoned to sprint for the train earlier that day. I respond to my co-workers' emails, who are even more distressed since I haven't responded in over three hours (unacceptable for a global law firm - they're always on duty).

- **10:00 p.m.:** Close my laptop (tomorrow's another day). Leave the dishes for my husband to wash while I pack up everything Beckett and I need the next day. Finally, I take a quick shower and collapse into bed.

- **12:00 a.m.:** Awaken to the sounds of my

hungry little guy who just realized I snuck away while he slept. Nurse again. Get in as much sweet baby love as I can, while also longing desperately for sleep. Transfer him back to his crib.

- **3:00 a.m.:** Awaken (again) to the sounds of my hungry little guy (again), who is upset that I've left him (again). Lift him from his crib (again) and nurse him (again). I struggle to hang onto consciousness.
- **5:00 a.m.:** Lather, rinse, repeat.

In just a few months, life had become one endless blur. All I could do was try to keep up with the demands of work, motherhood, and life, and I was even failing at that. I was burned out, though I hadn't realized it at the time.

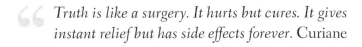

> *Truth is like a surgery. It hurts but cures. It gives instant relief but has side effects forever.* Curiane

Back to that lovely February afternoon. Joey and I were enjoying our first date in months. We needed this time together. The weekdays were a frantic sprint from the moment we woke up to the moment we went to bed. By the time the weekend rolled around, we were stressed and exhausted and looking down the barrel of a long list of household chores that needed our immediate attention.

Since we were both tired and overwhelmed with obligations that weren't particularly enjoyable or meaningful to us, we had turned on each other. We had started bickering about trivial things. We came to see each other as the enemy, the source of all of our struggles. Intellectually we knew better, but we didn't have anyone else to blame so we took it out on each other. We knew something had to change, but we didn't know what. We thought an afternoon on our own would be a good start.

We hired a sitter to watch Beckett so we could sneak away for an afternoon date. We ended up at a new restaurant in the area that had wood-fired pizza, an extensive wine list, and an outdoor fire pit. We grabbed some pizza, drinks, and just *connected* for the first time in months.

It was refreshing to relax with my favorite person in the world. No crying. No nursing. No responsibilities for the moment. Just great food, great wine, and great conversation.

Little did I know our lives were about to change forever.

———

Joey paid our bill and we headed for the parking lot. I put the car in reverse to head home, but something stopped me. I switched the engine off. Without warning, I put my head in my hands and started to cry.

"Honey, what's wrong?" Joey was confused. I had an upbeat attitude all through lunch. These tears came out of nowhere.

I cried harder.

"Sarah, what's going on? Why are you crying?" His confusion escalated. He had no idea what was wrong with me.

Within just a few minutes, I was sobbing so hard I couldn't speak and I was shaking.

"Sarah, you're scaring me. What's wrong?" Looking back, I can imagine he rationalized this outburst as erratic new mom hormones, which I can't deny probably played at least a small part.

At that point, I had no words. I didn't know what to say. I

was just... *sad*. And scared. And hopeless. And exhausted. And pissed off. And resentful — about *everything*.

On the surface, my life was as close to perfect as it gets. We lived in one of the most beautiful cities in the world. I had a well-paying job I loved. I worked with people I respected and who valued my contributions. My husband was supportive and caring and loyal and funny. And he loved me to bits. He even *washed dishes*.

Our son was healthy and growing by leaps and bounds every day. We had financial security, a whole group of incredible friends, and fun vacations planned with our extended family. The weather was 70 degrees. In *February*.

His question was a reasonable one. What the hell was wrong with me? What could I possibly have to complain about? Our life was seemingly perfect.

After ten minutes or so, my cries started to subside. I took a few deep breaths and said the thing I never expected to say.

"Joey, I can't keep doing this."

"*What* can't you keep doing?" He was still confused.

"This. Our life. Working all the time. Never seeing our son. Never seeing you. Feeling like I'm *constantly going*, but I never really accomplish anything. I feel like a complete failure as a mom. I love my job and I love my team, but I'm killing myself trying to work the way I used to. You and I fight more than we ever have. Everything is just so intense now. Life is just *hard*. I never sleep. I don't get to see my friends or do anything that *feels good*. My life now consists of nothing but chores and breastfeeding and work and sitting on a train I hate. Most of all, I feel like a *terrible* mom. I'm never there for Beckett. He gets twelve hours of quality time with a bunch of strangers at daycare, and I get to see him for 30 minutes at night when he's cranky and tired and mad that I've been gone all day. I *miss* him. I miss *you*... I miss *me*.

SARAH ARGENAL, MA, CPC

Nothing is working for any of us, and I just don't see it getting any better."

That's how I talk to Joey when I'm emotional, in diatribes. They're usually overwhelming for him, but (God love him) he listens. He was silent. He was taking what I've said to heart, but he was still working through how to respond. Before he got the chance, I continued.

"Joey, I know we've made some very conscious decisions about our life. We both wanted this baby. We love where we live. We love our jobs. We love that our family and friends are all nearby. We love the city, it's home to us both. But how are we ever going to get off this hamster wheel if we don't take a hard look at the choices we're making right now?"

I kept going. Once I get started, it's hard to stop until I get it all out.

"I love it here, but I don't know if I love it enough to sacrifice *everything*. Our marriage. Our relationship with our son. These years when he's little are precious, and I feel like I'm missing all of it. I already feel like it's going to be over in a blink of an eye. I can't take it. To make matters worse, even though I'm killing myself at work to keep up, I can tell my team is disappointed when I don't respond to emails right away or when I can't take on more projects. They're not used to me saying no. Even with how hard I'm working, I feel like I'm just not measuring up anymore."

I kept going...

"Joey, I thought I could juggle it all. I thought I could handle this. Or at the very least, I thought I'd be resourceful enough to figure out how to solve whatever problems came up. But I'm *not* good at this. I don't know how to be a mom and a wife and a friend and a daughter and a sister and have a career all at once. I hate who I am now. I'm bitchy and impatient and stressed out all the time. I can't keep up this charade of 'having it all together.' The truth is, I'm miserable. *You're* miserable. Beckett is miserable. When it comes down to it, our family is my priority and we're the ones getting screwed the most right now."

And going...

"Look, I know we're in a tough phase. Beckett is still young. We're just getting in our new groove. Everyone tells me it gets easier. But the things I don't like right now aren't going to get better. We both spend twenty hours a week on a train, at best. That's all time I could be spending with you and Beckett, or on my own relaxing, or with friends. We spend $1,500 a month on daycare alone. We live in a 2-bedroom condo an hour outside of the city. If we ever want another baby, we can't afford a bigger place or the cost of daycare for two kids, not without making our commute even longer and having to work harder. I'm just looking down the road, and I can't figure out what we can do to make things better, right now or in the future. I'm at a loss. I just don't know how to fix this."

My tears had calmed, but I was scared. I was terrified to let Joey in on all of this. Things had been... *touchy* between us for months. I felt like he was going to accuse me of pulling the rug out from under him. It wasn't long ago that we had taken marriage vows based on a certain reality. I felt like I was changing the rules on him all of a sudden. Everything we had built together no longer worked for me. I had no idea how he would respond.

After a few minutes of quiet reflection, Joey leaned over and gave me a big, warm hug. He wiped my tears and looked into my eyes.

"Sarah, I get it, and I agree. We can't keep going like this. I do think some things will change over time. But if you're not happy, I'm not okay with that. We're going to figure this out. I don't know what the answer is, but we'll figure it out together. We're a team, and we're going to do whatever we need to do for our family. I'm open to whatever happens. I'm here, and I'm not going anywhere."

And... more tears.

3

YOUR JOURNEY OUT OF BURNOUT
STARTS WITH A SMALL STEP

Joey's support in my need to explore a new approach to our life is something I'll always cherish. I was asking him to follow me - no, to *join* me - on a path of uncertainty and unpredictability, at a time when we already felt uncertain and our life was the most unpredictable it had ever been. Having a new baby had shaken the foundation of our lives in all sorts of different ways. So many things that had once seemed solid in our relationship and our life now seemed fragile and unclear. Instead of retreating to what was most familiar to us both, I was asking him to move *deeper* into the unknown. It was a big ask. To this day, I'm so grateful he was on board. He showed himself to be a true partner in my journey of self-discovery, even if he was craving stability and familiarity. I've thought a lot about that conversation over the years. It was a catalyst for change for us both as individuals and as a family.

While I was grateful at the time, I also wasn't sure if he realized how serious I was about making long-term changes in our lives. I knew we were both at risk of chalking my meltdown up to a hormone imbalance, exhaustion, or just a bad day. But I also knew things couldn't continue the way they had been. If we didn't make real changes soon, something was going to break in our life. I was certain of that. I was determined it wouldn't be our marriage or our health or our relationship with our son, or our career or friendships, or our financial security, or my self-worth. I wanted "it all," and the people who told me it was impossible just drove me to work that much harder to prove them wrong. I wasn't willing to settle for a lifetime of burnout and misery. Time was already passing way too quickly. My son was growing too fast. I wasn't going to miss another minute of it.

There had to be a way to find joy both at work *and* at home. I figured someone out there must have the answers. I couldn't be the only one feeling this way. So I did what I always do when I'm unsure about something in my life. I started researching.

I ordered every book I could find on Amazon about juggling work and motherhood. At the time, two big books about working motherhood were popular: Sheryl Sandberg's *Lean In* and Arianna Huffington's *Thrive*. I also came across a book called *Maxed Out* that seemed relevant. Beyond that, I wasn't finding too many books dedicated to helping burned out working moms. I had a three-hour commute on a train every day, so I started devouring these books. Here was my reaction to each of these popular books:

Lean In: Women, Work, and the Will to Lead by Sheryl Sandberg

I had a visceral reaction to this book. The main message I got from Sandberg was that I needed to work *harder*, to strive to achieve *more* at work than I ever had. I felt like she was telling me my career was meaningless if I wasn't climbing the ladder to be a C-level executive in a major corporation. I immediately felt shamed and exhausted. I was trying to find a way to step *back* from my career just a little bit, to spend more time with my family and on myself. Sandberg was telling me I needed to do the opposite. Even Sandberg, who became a single mom after the sudden and tragic death of her husband a few years later, has backtracked on some of the advice she offered in her first book. But the movement she ignited has persisted: to disparage working moms who decide to scale back in their career as their priorities change.

Thrive: The Third Metric to Redefining Success and Creating a Life of Well-Being, Wisdom, and Wonder **by Arianna Huffington**

I enjoyed this book a little more than *Lean In*. Arianna was at least acknowledging the fact that burnout was a real problem among working mothers, and she offered some practical solutions to combat it. She also encouraged CEOs to make some changes to the work environment they provided to better support the physical and mental wellness of their employees. I think her message has resonated around the world, and I'm grateful for her leadership in this area. But still, her message was geared toward CEOs and essentially absolved lower-level workers from making changes until their company leaders did. I couldn't wait for my global law firm to integrate her message into our office culture, where burnout and workaholism was baked into the culture. Her message offered me hope, but no immediate relief.

Maxed Out: American Moms on the Brink by **Katrina Alcorn**

This book resonated with me on many different levels. A new mom went back to work at her startup in downtown San Francisco, which is where I was living and working when I read this book, too. She had roughly the same commute I did, a demanding job similar to my own, and felt like a failure in just about every area of her life, just like I did. She struggled with sexism and people devaluing her contributions at work as her personal responsibilities expanded. I devoured this book, dying to get to the end where she would tell me how she *finally* figured out how to juggle everything in a way that I could apply in my own life. Not to give the ending away (spoiler alert), but that wasn't the conclusion she came to. She did find some peace and happiness, ultimately. But first, she had a nervous breakdown, took a year off from work, and shifted into a quieter life of part-time freelance writing.

All that buildup and the lesson I learned was: *Sorry, there's just no way to keep the career you worked so hard for. If you want to be a good mom (heck, if you want to avoid a complete nervous breakdown), you're going to have to leave the corporate sector.* Not exactly the inspiration I was looking for. I wasn't willing to give up the career I had built over twenty years. I had to find another way.

My research wasn't going well. I hadn't found anything that would tell me how to enjoy my life as a working mom without having to sacrifice either my family, my career, or myself. At that point, the overriding message I received was that I would have to choose one area of my life over another. I refused to accept that answer. *All* of these aspects of my life were important to me: my health, my marriage, my relationship with my son, my career, my friendships, my family. No matter how many times I evaluated my life, I couldn't find anything I was willing to sacrifice.

Out of desperation, I realized I would have to dig a little deeper. I put a lifetime of research skills to the test and expanded my search. That's when I finally started to get somewhere.

> You don't just wake up and become the butterfly. Growth is a process. Rupi Kour

WHAT IS BURNOUT?

I didn't have the words for it at the time, but I've come to understand my breakdown with Joey as the result of prolonged burnout. "Burnout" is a word that's tossed around liberally in our society. But I've found that many people don't have a clear view of what burnout is, or how it really impacts their daily lives. I certainly didn't.

The World Health Organization classified "work-related burnout" as a medical phenomenon in 2019. While they don't refer to it as a medical disorder itself, they do acknowledge that burnout produces symptoms that influence people to seek treatment for a variety of other medical disorders, and as a result should be taken into account by medical professionals.

The World Health Organization defines work-related burnout as: *A syndrome conceptualized as resulting from chronic workplace stress that has not been successfully managed. It is characterized by three dimensions:*

- *feelings of energy depletion or exhaustion;*
- *increased mental distance from one's job, or*

feelings of negativism or cynicism related to one's job; and

- *reduced professional efficacy.*

While that begins to describe the challenges I faced as a working mom, it's woefully incomplete. There were many other symptoms that characterized my burnout experience. Here are some of the more obscure symptoms that were warning signs that I was struggling with burnout.

Physical Symptoms

- Chronic fatigue
- Lack of energy
- Sleep disorders such as over-tiredness or insomnia
- Headaches or migraines
- Distractibility and inability to focus
- Change in appetite leading to extreme weight gain or loss
- Increased illness or weakened immune system
- Chest pains or heart palpitations
- Muscle tension
- Dizziness
- Restlessness

Emotional Symptoms

- Anxiety
- Depression
- Dysthymia (low-level sense of sadness or disinterest in life)
- Overwhelm at common, everyday activities

- Inability to cope with challenging situations
- Guilt
- Anger or rage
- Cynicism or pessimism
- Apathy
- Tearfulness
- Forgetfulness

Relational Symptoms

- Increased conflict with loved ones
- Distancing, detachment, or disconnection
- Impatience with others
- Questioning viability of relationships
- Reduction in effectiveness at home or work
- Lack of trust in others
- Isolation

Lifestyle Symptoms

- Inability to identify and focus on priorities
- Confusion around values and internal purpose
- Doubt about my identity and life purpose
- Poor performance at work or home
- Loss of productivity
- Loss of motivation
- A sense of powerlessness
- Disorganization

These conditions were all hard to recognize as symptoms of burnout because they were so common throughout many stages of my life. They were also universal among the attorneys I was surrounded by, as well as other working parents I knew. Just about all of these issues were *normal* in my reality, which just highlights the insidious role they played on my journey to despair.

As I continued my research, I finally started to find some golden nuggets of wisdom that made a difference.

———

ESSENTIALISM

I was standing in line at Starbucks before work one morning when I learned the lesson that finally launched my pivot to a different kind of life. In his book, *Essentialism: The Disciplined Pursuit of Less*, Greg McKeown identified something I had been doing my whole adult life that was the root of many of my struggles.

When I started my career in 1999, email was just beginning to become a part of work life. I received maybe 20 or 30 emails a day. The pace of life was slower. Expectations were more reasonable, even in the litigation field. Twenty years later, it was common for me to receive upwards of 500 emails a day, most of which included a new task for me to complete or respond to personally.

As a dedicated legal professional, I had been trained to reply to every email instantly, and certainly within ten minutes at most. I was also encouraged to respond, "I'm on it!" regardless of what was asked of me. No complaints, no excuses. It was my job to find a way to get it all done, no matter what. I had resources I could rely on, but it was up to me to figure out how to manage everything. As the number of emails (not to mention voicemails, text messages, and chat messages) increased throughout my career, the pace of my life became more frantic as well.

Then I added a baby to the mix, and my life quickly became unsustainable.

McKeown describes two ways to manage this level of demand on our time, energy, and attention: 1) check out completely and stop trying to keep up altogether, or 2) become hyperactive to stay on top of it all. Since my identity at the time was tied inextricably to my ability to be helpful, I naturally defaulted the latter. Identifying that my people-pleasing tendencies were playing a part in my burnout led me to realize I had to make some changes. From that moment on, I became more mindful of the projects I committed to, both in my work and personal life. I became discerning about where I focused my resources. I stopped accepting guilt when I couldn't do everything for everyone around me. I relentlessly focused on the areas that *would* make the most significant impact both at work and at home, and either delegated or asked for support in the other areas.

Slowly but surely, life started to become more manageable.

———

CONSCIOUS PARENTING

I went into parenthood thinking my job as a mom was to mold my baby into a hardworking, respectful, well-adjusted child. My focus as a mom was very much on finding the perfect parenting plan and executing that ideal plan to get a specific outcome. Every parenting book I read reinforced the idea that my child's well-being and success was *entirely* dependent on my performance as a parent. I bought into the message that my baby's future relied on my *doing parenting well*. As a result, I mainly experienced parenting as a slew of new responsibilities heaped onto my already overflowing to-do list. I tried applying my organizational and project management skills from my professional career to my role as a parent so I could be a "good mom."

Then I came across an interview Oprah did with Shefali Tsabary on her show, *Super Soul Sunday*. As a child psychologist and author of *The Conscious Parent*, Tsabary approaches parenthood in a completely different way than I had ever contemplated. She helps parents view children as a reflection of the areas of growth they need to work on *within themselves*. She encourages parents to utilize the challenges of parenthood to heal their *own* psychological trauma to become *whole* themselves.

After reading this book, I started to view my role as a "parent" as a fundamental part of my *identity*, rather than a list of behaviors I needed to execute. I started to see my son as his own person who would develop and grow in his own way and at his own pace. I shifted into being more of a facilitator and coach than dictator. Slowly, I removed the self-imposed pressure to mold my child in any particular way. Instead, I learned to *respond* to his unique needs with intention and a sense of detached compassion.

I began to focus on nurturing my relationship with my son, above all else. I let go of the concept of parenting as a series of actions I had to take to produce a successful child. I still provided a consistent routine and firm boundaries, but the *tone* of our exchanges evolved. I learned to view conflict and power struggles as clues to *my own* shortcomings or fears or life lessons. Understanding parenthood as a vehicle for *my* personal growth has made my journey as a parent a fascinating exploration. My uncertainty, shame, and anxiety also evaporated when I let go of the sky-high stakes of raising a perfect human.

———

DOWNSHIFTING

Now I was getting somewhere. My perspective was shifting in small ways that were making a big difference on my stress levels and my ability to connect to those I loved. It was around this time I came across a book called *Work, Pause, Thrive: How to Pause for Parenthood Without Ruining Your Career* by Lisen Stromberg. This was the first book I read that reinforced my instinct to step back from the hyper-focus on my career to be more present for my family and myself. For the first time, I got the message that being an engaged and involved mom didn't have to come at the expense of my career, or vice versa. I also realized my career didn't have to look the way it always had. I could get creative.

I had resisted the message that opting out of my career when my kids were young would be a catastrophic mistake. I knew I wanted to continue to work in some capacity, but I also knew I didn't want my work to consume as much of my time and energy as it did before I became a mom. This book helped me envision a new lifestyle that worked for my family and me in this new season of our lives. I started to consider how I could ramp up and downshift in my work at different times, depending on what was going on in other areas of my life. I realized that there are a lot of different ways to have a career in the modern world. I could contribute my professional skills in a variety of forms. I could also adapt and respond appropriately based on the changing circumstances in my life.

———

WHAT'S IN YOUR TOOLBOX?

Even after all of my research, I never found the Working Parent Bible I was looking for. Instead, I started gathering little nuggets of perspective from a variety of sources that made a small difference in my life. I accumulated a unique collection of tools for *my* working parent toolbox, which I could implement as necessary. I would come to rely on these tools to varying degrees in all different areas of my life. There were also plenty of resources I found that didn't work for me, though. I started to become comfortable letting go of what didn't serve me to make more room for what did, trusting I could always reach out for those tools again in the future if circumstances changed.

In the meantime, Joey and I were having an ongoing conversation about our life. We made some small changes early on that made a tiny, but noticeable, difference in our stress levels, our communication skills, and our approach to working parent life. We started to evolve our understanding not only of ourselves as individuals, but as a married couple and as parents, too. Our identities were shifting, little by little. We were growing into healthier and happier versions of ourselves, very slowly but very deliberately.

4

HOW DID WE GET HERE?

I've been interviewed for different podcasts and parenting articles over the last few years. One question I always inevitably get is, "Why are working parents struggling so much?" When I first started this work, I thought the primary source of the struggle working parents faced could be reduced to a few different things:

- A need for better time management skills.
- A lack of a reliable self-care practice.
- An inability to set healthy boundaries with others.
- Perfectionism or other people-pleasing tendencies.

Over time I've discovered there's a lot more happening, both within ourselves and in our society at large, that impacts a working parent's ability to overcome burnout and create a fulfilling life without sacrificing what matters most to them. There are some complex developments that need to be understood on a deeper level before we can implement effective solutions. Yet, most of these elements aren't acknowledged in the discussion on work-life balance or burnout. We're missing the big picture, which hinders our efforts to create better lives for ourselves once we're parents.

> *I wish I'd had the courage to live a life true to myself, not the life others expected of me.* Bronnie Ware in her book, "5 Regrets of the Dying"

I've found that there are three broad categories of obstacles that hold working parents back from enjoying their lives in modern society:

1. **Internal Obstacles** hold us back from within ourselves.
2. **Interpersonal Obstacles** hold us back in our relationships and communities.
3. **Cultural Obstacles** hold us back through societal systems and norms.

In the next few chapters, I'll offer a quick overview of these psychological, interpersonal, and cultural obstacles. While I don't think we need to be experts in any of these areas to break free of their hold on us, I do believe it's helpful to understand the broader context of the burnout issue before we dive into what to do about it. I've observed most of these challenges through thousands of first-hand conversations I've had with working parents and experts. However, many of these insights are also drawn from books, articles, studies, and podcasts I've been exposed to over the years. In those cases, I'll reference supporting materials in the Recommended

Resources in the Bonus Library, in case you want to dive deeper into any of these topics on your own.

I encourage you to investigate any of the elements that sound familiar to you. There are experts in all of these subjects who know much more about these areas than I do. It's worth exploring if you suspect these obstacles may be contributing to your experience. The more you understand about what's impacting your life, and *how* it's presenting itself in your life, the better equipped you'll be to respond in a way that works best for you.

5

THE INTERNAL REASONS BURNOUT PERSISTS

The internal reasons burnout persists in the life of a working parent comes from within each of us. These obstacles have nothing to do with the people around us. They have everything to do with patterns, beliefs, and behaviors that operate on a conscious and subconscious level in our lives. The following list includes some of the most common internal reasons for burnout I've come across in my work and research. It's not an exhaustive list and I don't go into great depth on any of these issues. My goal here is to give you a broad idea of the types of limitations to joy that might be hiding in plain sight in your life.

MYTHS AND BELIEFS

The first and biggest hurdle we have to overcome as working parents if we want more fulfilling lives are the myths and false beliefs that hold us back from change. Until we overcome these myths, there's no point in even trying to change our circumstances. When our internal psychology holds us back, it doesn't matter what's happening in the world around us. We have control over our thoughts and beliefs, *if* we investigate them. Our false beliefs need to be identified, understood, and released in order to move toward a healthier lifestyle.

Here are just a few of the most prominent myths I've uncovered through my work over the years:

This is what I signed up for.

A few years ago, I conducted a survey of working parents in the legal field, since it's an environment where burnout is prevalent and I had such an intimate experience with it myself. Every single person I talked to claimed some variation of the same thing:

- *Well, this is just how it is.*
- *The best I can do is just get through it.*
- *I can't complain, I knew what I was getting into when I chose this career.*

Not one person in my survey realized they had a *choice* in eliminating the stress or frustration they felt. They were all utterly resigned to the fact that their life was destined to be unfulfilling as they juggled a career in law and parenthood.

Over the years, I've seen this belief surface in many different industries. It's destroying our ability to address the problem in any sort of real way. We don't even realize it is a problem. We've normalized dysfunction and misery.

I should know how to do this.

Another pervasive myth I hear from ambitious professionals, in particular, is *I should know how to do this.* The thinking with anyone who's had some success in life seems to be, "I'm a smart, capable person. There's a ton of information out there. I can figure this out."

This might be true for some people, but what I find is that working parents don't have a whole lot of extra time or energy. So when they try to overcome whatever their most prominent problem of the day is, they either ask their closest friends for advice or scan the most prominent self-help articles on their social media feed.

The trouble with this approach is that they aren't even sure what the real, underlying source of their pain is. It's usually not just one thing they're dealing with. There's often a combination of factors that are all working in tandem. They're grasping at straws to find some relief from the symptoms they feel. But they never actually address the *root cause* of the problem, which means they stay trapped in burnout mode.

What we see on the surface is often just the tip of the iceberg. We're dealing with a tangled web of circumstances and feelings and lifelong unconscious patterns of behavior. It's not about intellect, or work ethic, or authenticity, or even having grit. There's a lot more complexity to it. No one should feel like they should *just know* how to do this.

Balance isn't possible.

This is the saddest myth of all because the people who believe this – and the numbers are growing – have given up hope that a happier and healthier life exists. They buy into the message that they *can't* be happier, it's just not possible. It makes sense because everywhere you look, working parents appear to be miserable. People are sinking deeper and deeper into hopelessness.

But there are examples everywhere (I'm just one of them) that you can have a thriving and stimulating career, a happy marriage, a strong bond with your kids, time for yourself, and a deep sense of purpose and satisfaction in your life. That doesn't mean you don't experience struggle at times, or that your life is perfect. It just means your *overall* feelings about your life include contentment, peace, and joy. It's time to reject this myth that balance (or integration, or work/life blend, or harmony, or whatever phrase you prefer) isn't possible.

I'm too busy to find a different way.

Every working parent I work with believes they don't have enough time to prioritize creating a more fulfilling life on top of all of the other demands they're juggling every day. This belief is legitimate because most people are trying to do way too much with no support. We've lost the villages that used to make being a parent easier. Many of us are doing it all on our own. We tell ourselves, "I don't have time to be happy." It seems easier to power through our day than to slow down, even for a short while, to figure out a way to reclaim control of our lives. On the surface, it seems to require less effort to kick the can down the road and just focus on getting through *this* day.

But we need to make the time. We no longer live in an era that will support us having a reasonably paced life unless we insist upon it for ourselves. We live in a new world that is relentlessly demanding. I think we can assume the noise will never subside at this point. But we don't need to comply with every request heaped upon us. We don't need to be so cooperative. We don't need to engage with everyone and everything that competes for our attention. Instead, we need to get *clear* about what we're willing to give and what's important to us, and then set clear boundaries around our time and energy with that in mind.

I can't be successful if I don't hustle.

There's a widespread myth that you can't be successful if you aren't willing to hustle. The world has gotten more competitive, so we feel like we can't afford to take a moment to rest. Like a never-ending game of musical chairs, we're afraid to be the last ones standing when the music stops. So we keep moving and hope we don't fall behind. But this "no pain, no gain" mantra is eating us alive.

Working nonstop *may* get you the results you want in the end, but at what cost? How much are you willing to sacrifice on the journey to that elusive destination? Are you sacrificing your physical and mental well-being? Are you sacrificing your marriage? Are you sacrificing your relationship or quality time with your kids? Are you sacrificing friendships or other meaningful relationships? Are you sacrificing your happiness? Your values? We're trained to believe that hard work will lead to success. But the question is, how do *you* define success? If you leave a wake of misery on the path to success, is it worth it?

Being in demand means I'm important and valuable.

This is a myth I bought into for most of my life. For too long, I thought my worth depended on how helpful I was to others. I wanted love in my life (as we all do), and I thought the only way to secure that love was by doing things for other people. In my quest for love and approval from others, I lost touch with just about everything important to *me*: my values, my relationships, my health, and the activities that gave my life meaning. Eventually, I had to let go of the belief that being busy was a reflection of how important I was and start looking for that source of love within myself.

Time management is the key to overcoming burnout.

Every time I talk to a working parent about their struggles, they inevitably point to their lack of time as the source of their troubles. They think if they can just become more productive, their problems will cease. Once they achieve optimal efficiency, then they'll have time for all of the obligations that have piled onto their to-do list. They'll have time for their families. They'll have time to relax at the end of the day without the guilt of a messy kitchen or unmade school lunches. But working harder and faster just perpetuates the frantic pace of their life, and they still aren't finding fulfillment within the time they save. That extra time just gets filled with more work.

I'm not strong enough to find out the truth.

This one may not resonate on the surface, but take a moment to think about it. Do you avoid looking too closely at what's hard in your life? Do you naturally turn away from what you're most afraid of? Do you avoid challenges because you're worried you'll crack under pressure, or do you lean into discomfort? Do negative emotions feel overwhelming, and best left locked in the deep recesses of your mind? Do you see challenges as an opportunity for growth, or clear reasons why you haven't excelled further in life?

Survival mode is perpetuated when we sweep the real source of our struggles under the rug. But we can only avoid those struggles for so long before we start to experience anxiety, depression, isolation, physical illness, broken relationships, or a loss of our sense of self. Survival mode seems like the answer to your struggles in the moment, but over time it just compounds the problems you're unwilling to face. If you're ready to start doing the deep work of examining the dark corners of your life, this book outlines the baby steps to get there.

Those are just a few of the myths I've seen that hold working parents back from pursuing a more fulfilling lifestyle. If you're thinking any of those things, this is a heads-up that these are just myths. They are false beliefs. They aren't real. You can let them go and find a better way, starting right now.

 Owning our story and loving ourselves through that process is the bravest thing that we'll ever do.
Brene Brown, Ph.D., LCSW

OTHER PSYCHOLOGICAL BARRIERS

Myths and false beliefs aren't the only internal obstacles to fulfillment I've come across. Here are some other internal limitations I've discovered within myself and many working parents I support. This isn't a comprehensive list and these issues may or may not apply to you. Rather than imposing these challenges on you where they may not exist, my hope is that this list will kickstart an exploration into the unique psychological barriers that may be holding *you* back in your own life.

My identity was outdated.

Becoming a parent shattered everything I thought I knew about myself. My identity went through a transformation, a deepening. I let go of old parts of myself. I took on new roles in my relationships and my life. I started to understand myself in different ways. I continue to face unfamiliar circumstances, which requires new skills and perspectives to work through. I am still learning to integrate who I *used to be* with who I am *becoming*.

For a long time, I was too busy to explore my own shifting identity in any useful way. That's when I was most suscep-tible to outside influences. My sense of self was continually shifting, and I didn't understand it deeply enough to guide my choices, behavior, or beliefs. I relied almost exclusively on experts, "gurus," and opinions of friends and family for guid-ance. I lost trust in myself to do what was best for myself, my family, and our future. I was living from the *outside in*, not the other way around. I was prioritizing other people's agendas and values above my own. This contributed to that feeling of a lack of control over my own life. My ability to reclaim my time, energy and sense of happiness came directly from a deepening of my sense of *self*. Once I had that solid sense of self, I began a practice of working from that center as often as possible.

My priorities and values changed.

Before I had children, my career was my top priority and the core of my entire identity. When work demands piled up,

I just worked harder and faster to get things done. Then I became a mom, and my old approach no longer worked. I was juggling too much, but the thought of putting work on the back burner was completely foreign to me. I didn't know how to do that. Things started falling through the cracks both at work and at home. I knew my family was what I valued most, but my actions weren't reflecting my new values. Worst of all, the harder I tried to power through all of my work so that I could focus on what I actually valued most, the faster I drove myself into burnout. I eventually realized I had to clarify my *current* values, and prioritize different aspects of my life based on my updated values.

Ongoing uncertainty.

As parents, we confront new challenges on a daily basis. This persistent state of change can be disorienting. It can lead to varying levels of fear and uncertainty. My natural reaction in these situations is to search for stability. I spent a lot of time searching in vain for a manual that would tell me exactly what to do to reclaim control of my life. I was enticed by promises of a quick fix that would finally offer some permanence in my life. Overcoming burnout for good required that I learn how to accept, and even embrace, the unpredictability of working parenthood.

Compartmentalization.

We increasingly exist in distinct but separate "silos" in our lives. Each aspect of our lives requires a different part of us to show up. Many of us reveal one side of ourselves at work. Another to our best friend. Another to our neighbors. Another to the networking group we joined. We bring a different side of ourselves to the book club we meet with once a month. Our kids and spouse see yet another side of us.

Today, with the emergence of digital connectivity and rising expectations of instant gratification, it's getting harder and harder to partition one area of my life from the others. When I try to, I find I exchange one hat for another to deal with different circumstances in my life. All of that context switching drains our energy. I've discovered that I need to show up as my *whole self* in all areas of my life in order to feel sane. When I don't show up as my whole self, I feel fractured and conflicted. I'm not truly present. That's when I numb out and miss the deeper layers of my life experience.

Intellectual entertainment.

We have no shortage of information in the 21st century. We have access to everything we need to know at our fingertips. But many of us didn't grow up this way. If you came of age before the 1990s as I did, you had an "analog" childhood. We were encouraged to learn a particular set of facts in school and rely on that basis of knowledge throughout our daily lives. At that time, the volume of information available to us was manageable and easier to consume at a reasonable rate.

Now we're adults raising children of our own, and we haven't developed the skill of filtering out the barrage of information we're exposed to on a moment-to-moment basis. We feel compelled to consume as much information as possible so we can refer to it as needed in the future. We're not used to waiting to learn information until it will be immediately useful. So we take it all in and store it for later use, which is what we were trained to do. That knowledge accumulates, and we feel overwhelmed with facts, options, and ideals. We don't do anything with most of what we learn. Or, for those of us who do implement what we learn, it only sticks for a short time. We lose it when life gets complicated. At that point, we naturally revert to our default habits.

The information we consume is mostly useless, but the consumption itself clogs our minds and drains our energy. In fact, recent studies show that this type of passive mental consumption of non-essential information is actually causing brain damage in humans.

Real change is scary.

This is the hardest internal hurdle for most working parents to overcome. We're bombarded with promises of a quick fix to any problem we have these days. We have an endless news feed on social media that will tell us the secret to a happy life. All we have to do is change this *one little thing* about ourselves, and we'll have lasting success and joy. Just save some extra time, get more sleep, meditate, exercise, connect more with your spouse, focus on self-care, or try this new product to lose weight, and your life will be perfect. Easy as pie, right?

This isn't necessarily *bad* advice. It's just *incomplete*. It's a compelling promise, but the truth is that true fulfillment is far more complex, and it comes from a different source. I've discovered that all of the things I want as a working parent - a healthy and loving marriage, confidence as a parent, connection with my kids, respectful and positive friendships, stimulating and purposeful work, time for myself to do the things that are meaningful to me, and some quiet time to enjoy the life I've created - all of those things come from one thing, and none of those things are possible without it: *self-awareness.*

Understanding myself on as many levels as possible is the

antidote to so many of the problems I experience as a working mother. As someone who has specialized in personal development over the last twenty years, I know this is where we need to begin to turn our societal burnout problems around. But digging below the surface, shining a light in the dark corners of our psyche, can be intimidating. It feels like opening Pandora's box. So, we keep our fears locked up, hoping they'll go away... but they never do.

———

This list of internal barriers may or may not sound familiar to you. You may be able to relate to some of these subliminal struggles and not others. You may have a whole other list of internal reasons why burnout persists in your life. It's worth the effort to identify and explore the psychological dynamics that may be holding *you* back. Until you do, it doesn't matter what other solutions you try to integrate into your life. They'll always fall short.

6

THE INTERPERSONAL REASONS
BURNOUT PERSISTS

Internal barriers will hold us back from enjoying our experience as working parents, but our relationships also play a significant role in our experience. Here are just a few interpersonal obstacles to fulfillment I've discovered over the years.

Parenting puts a strain on a marriage.

The first few years after welcoming a baby into the family can be one of the most stressful periods of a couple's life. Exhaustion. Added stress. Family roles and dynamics shift. Different parenting styles reveal the need for more cooperation and new communication skills. There's a *lot* to navigate in those early parenting years. Everyone is going through a significant life transition that brings with it added uncertainty and stress. But this relationship is also the foundation of your family. The more you can strengthen your bond with your partner in these early parenting years, the more you can use this period of transition to create a robust foundation for your family going forward.

Moms struggle with mental load.

Women make up half of the workforce today, but they continue to bear a disproportionate portion of household and family responsibilities. According to a study commissioned by Bright Horizons Family Solutions®:

- Breadwinning mothers are three times more likely than breadwinning fathers to be keepers of their children's schedules and responsible for them getting to activities and appointments (76% vs. 22%).
- They're three times more likely to volunteer at school (63% vs. 19%).
- They're nearly twice as likely to make sure all family responsibilities are handled (71% vs. 38%).

Men are becoming more engaged in childcare and household matters to be sure, but the weight is still disproportionally on moms to carry the burden. In addition, dads who *do* try to take advantage of flexible work options often experience the same type of "motherhood penalty," stigma, and lack of career mobility that women do. Even as families struggled to adapt to self-isolation orders during the coronavirus quarantine, women endured a majority of family responsibilities. So far, we haven't found a way to entirely integrate men into home life in a way that will dramatically relieve the burden on women at home. We're getting closer in a lot of ways, but we still have more to do.

Dads want to become more involved at home, but they lack a relevant model.

As parents, we're influenced by what we observed in our own childhood. It's often all we know about parenthood. Until recently, that typically looked like mom at home dealing with everything related to the household and child-care, and dad responsible for making the family income. This is an incredibly important variable that I don't think gets enough attention in parenting conversations today. Many dads are open and ready to engage at home. But when they do, moms find they have a hard time welcoming dad into "their domain." Many women forget that it might take a little training and a lot of patience when things don't happen as they'd like. Many dads are afraid to step on mom's toes or they may feel incapable, so they resist getting involved as much as they need to. This dynamic is compounded in homosexual, single, or other non-traditional family structures. It can be tricky to find a division of responsibilities that works for your unique family, but it's worth the struggle.

 Your outer life mirrors your inner belief system.
Shefali Tsabary, Ph.D.

The first five years of a child's life are critical.

It's well documented that the first five years of a child's life are crucial to our kids' development, well-being, and the overall trajectory of their lives. For modern parents, these are also the years when we're the most sleep-deprived, adjusting to our new role as a parent while also figuring out how to juggle our family responsibilities with ongoing pressure at work. If we don't get a handle on how to manage parenthood effectively in their early years, it's easy to develop unhealthy habits, damaging patterns, and ineffective solutions that do more harm than good in the long-term.

Dr. Nadine Burke Harris, the first surgeon general of California, has discovered a direct link between what she refers to as adverse childhood experiences ("ACEs") and the broader societal issues we see today, such as addiction, bullying, incarceration, anxiety, depression, poverty, and physical illness. In her book, *The Deepest Well: Healing the Long-Term Effects of Childhood Adversity*, and in a study on youth trauma, Dr. Harris and the Centers for Disease Control and Prevention specify 10 categories of stressful or traumatic events that can impact a child's life. These 10 categories include experiences such as abuse, parental incarceration, addiction, or separation or divorce. Some of the risk factors also include things which may seem relatively benign but actually *do* have a significant impact, such as:

- A parent's lack of parenting skills or understanding of their child's individual needs.
- Substance abuse or mental health issues including depression or anxiety.
- Parental thoughts or emotions that tend to support or justify maltreatment behaviors.
- Family stress, separation, or divorce.
- Poor parent-child relationships and negative interactions.

Dr. Harris explains that what we experience in childhood changes our system on a *physiological* as well as a psychological level, and it has a profound effect that lasts a lifetime.

There was a part of me that was reluctant to include this

section in this book, because the last thing I want is for busy working parents who are already burned out to feel like every little mistake they make will ruin their child's life. That pressure is already an inescapable part of modern parenthood. That's not the point here. We can absolutely make mistakes without doing lasting damage to our kids' lives. Open communication, honesty, and respect for our kids can heal a lot of wounds.

That said, it is important that you're aware of the reality that most parents instinctively know; we have a *big* influence on our kids' development. When we're frantic and distracted, our children pick up on that energy. When our marriage is strained because we're overwhelmed, our kids feel a lack of security that sticks with them for life. When we prioritize what's *urgent* over what's *important* day after day, our kids internalize that as well. When our rage is triggered by normal but inconvenient childhood behavior, our kids internalize fear and can become confused about their value as human beings.

This doesn't mean we need to be superhuman. It doesn't mean we can't have priorities besides our children. It doesn't mean we can't have bad days. But it does mean it's essential to be mindful about the environment we're exposing our children to, and how that environment might affect them over time. The little things matter more than you might think.

Parental mental health is declining.

Our mental health as parents has a significant impact on our experience as working parents, too. According to multiple studies from the Anxiety and Depression Association of America, Blue Cross Blue Shield, Centers for Disease Control, the Department of Education, and the American

Psychological Association, the rates of anxiety, depression, bullying, and suicide have skyrocketed over the last twenty years in the United States. The technology-obsessed, achievement-oriented culture we've developed in recent decades is leading to a lack of connection, intrinsic motivation, emotional regulation, and empathy in society. When we're too busy to maintain our own mental well-being, we're unable to manage our lives effectively. Small stressors become magnified and seem impossible to overcome.

There's an undeniable link between parents' mental health and the growing number of children who report chronic anxiety, depression, stress, and burnout as well. Kids entering middle school and beyond have adopted our frantic, distracted, and numbing-out behaviors to cope with the pressure to succeed. As parents discovered after the sudden closure of schools and cancellation of all activities due to the threat of coronavirus, children are often calmer and healthier with a simpler lifestyle that prioritizes connection and play over an obsession with achievement and constant judgment.

If you're reading this book, I know you've been doing your best with the resources you have. But your health matters, and parents today have trouble prioritizing their mental and emotional health. There are too many demands, and it seems like your needs are the only ones that can be delayed. Please understand, your mental well-being is a *critical* component to overcoming burnout and enjoying life as a working parent. This is where it all starts. This is a reality we need to start paying attention to if we're ever going to find the incentive to make real changes in our lives. Giving our kids the best chance at life doesn't come from extracurricular activities, *Baby Einstein* movies, or early education reading drills. Most of what we're told we need to do to be "good parents" is just complicating our lives and contributing to our burnout. The more we focus on becoming healthy and happy *ourselves*, the more we model and inspire that behavior for the people around us as well, most of all our children.

Communication vs. Connection.

Humans are social beings. We rely on connection with others for health and happiness. There's a difference between *communication* and *connection*, though, which has gotten lost as technology has taken over our lives.

The rise of the internet and social media undoubtedly provides many opportunities for interaction. Over the last several months, technology has been a crucial tool to stay in touch with loved ones and colleagues as we navigated a near-global social distancing policy. We can talk to billions of people around the world whenever we choose. There are indisputably benefits to that, especially when we're feeling isolated or lonely. What we've also discovered throughout this long quarantine period though, is it's an inadequate substitute for in-person connection with others.

Social media has replaced face-to-face interactions with a growing majority of people. Relying solely on social media to further our relationships can limit our production of oxytocin, a hormone that causes us to feel bonded with others. Oxytocin increases our feelings of love and trust. Intimacy relies on oxytocin. When we communicate with other people on social media, the quick dopamine hit we get can trick us into believing we're fostering deep relationships with other people. But if we don't engage with people *off-line* as well, we experience counterfeit intimacy rather than *real* connection, which isn't as deeply fulfilling.

The more we rely on social media and other technology for our relationships, the less time and energy we have to

SARAH ARGENAL, MA, CPC

foster the types of intimate relationships that fulfill our innate human needs for connection, love, and belonging. We may feel less entitled to reach out for support from the people we're connected to online than we would from people with whom we're more intimate in real life. I suspect most of us will appreciate our ability to engage with our friends, family, neighbors, and colleagues even more once we're allowed to fully re-integrate into society. But old habits die hard, and it may be easy to fall back into the habit of prioritizing communication over true connection. Make sure you're using technology and social media as a tool to *reinforce* your in-person or long-distance relationships, rather than *replace* them.

7

THE CULTURAL REASONS BURNOUT PERSISTS

E ven after we overcome these internal and interpersonal obstacles, we're faced with some very real structural barriers in society. Most of our institutional systems were built in a different era when women generally stayed home to nurture the children, and men focused their attention outside the home. The family structure has become more egalitarian over the last several decades, but social evolution on a broader scale is taking longer to catch up. We're still very much in transition. Here are just a few of the cultural elements we need to navigate and improve in order to cement a healthier way of life for working parents in the modern world.

Hyper-focus on productivity

Modern society moves at a breakneck pace. I talk to working parents every day, both moms and dads, who tell me they are drowning. We haven't yet developed the skills to filter and respond effectively to the constant flood of demands we encounter every day. We don't know how to set our *own* pace and work from that basis. This is a big problem. Our ongoing desire to optimize every moment is driving our collective descent into burnout. Our obsession with achieving maximum efficiency is having a long-term effect on our species' health. It's time we accept that we're *humans*, not machines.

Economic instability

In 2008, the United States and many countries around the world experienced the worst economic collapse since the Great Depression in 1929. Millions of qualified professionals lost their jobs, careers, and (for many) the primary source of their purpose and identity. College students went into considerable debt for a degree, and then found it impossible to find a job that offered a living wage. Many low-wage workers lost their livelihoods altogether and were forced to depend on government programs for survival. Those who were lucky enough to keep their jobs during this period experienced a growing sense of uncertainty, too. They survived several rounds of layoffs, but their survival wasn't guaranteed forever. These people and others experienced a sense of professional insecurity that's hard to shake, even if they were eventually able to find a comparable salary.

It wasn't long ago that our economy seemed strong and stable. The graduating class of 2020 was prepared to enter a robust workforce. Then the coronavirus began to spread around the world, and everything changed. We have all watched our stable economy disappear overnight as record numbers of workers file unemployment claims and businesses fold. But even before the coronavirus pandemic hit our cities, the economy wasn't all it seemed. Wages were stagnated. Many professionals had taken on the responsibilities of several workers without an increase in salary or adjusted expectations. Working parents felt vulnerable to job loss if they couldn't keep up the pace they demonstrated they were capable of before they had kids. Working parents have been trying to keep up with an unsustainable professional climate for over a decade, and our economy just became even more volatile. As I write this, the United States is headed into an even deeper recession than we endured in 2008, and perhaps even a depression. As we attempt to resume some measure of normal activity, the residual impact of economic collapse is likely to continue for many years, just as it did following 2008.

Income inequality

Many working parents followed a predictable path toward success early in their lives: work hard in school, go to college, get an entry-level job, and work your way up the corporate ladder to higher levels of management. As long as you got into a reputable college, you were pretty much guaranteed at least a middle-class lifestyle.

Today, the standard life path isn't leading to the kind of success it used to. Getting into a respectable college that will lead to job security has become increasingly competitive. We as parents feel the pressure to prepare our kids for college at earlier and earlier ages so they have a fighting chance to earn a living wage. The unemployment rate was low until early 2020, but those unemployment numbers are skyrocketing and on track to become higher than they've been in almost a century. Even for professionals who are still employed, there are millions who don't earn enough to support their families on one income alone. They are forced to juggle more than one job just to stay afloat.

While wages have remained stagnant, other costs have increased. The cost of college has more than doubled over the last twenty years. Many working parents are not only paying off their own burdensome student loan debt, but they are also working hard to subsidize their kids' tuition when they can. Childcare costs, especially in urban areas where jobs are most prevalent, have ballooned. Healthcare costs have increased. The middle class is highly leveraged, struggling to pay off credit card and other debt.

According to a recent article in Forbes, a staggering 78% of people live paycheck to paycheck, including those making over $100,000 per year in salary. Nearly 3 in 4 workers say they are in debt, and more than half think they always will be. More than 1 in 4 workers do not set aside any savings each month. And those numbers are all likely to worsen as we deal with a pandemic-related economic collapse.

With so many professionals living on the financial edge, a job loss in their family would be catastrophic. They feel trapped in work conditions that cause stress, exhaustion, and ultimately burnout. They don't believe they have the freedom to set boundaries around their time or limit the tasks they take on. The fear of getting fired is deep, so they put their head down and try to get through it all as quickly as possible.

Lack of media literacy

As modern parents raising the next generation in the post-digital age, we're faced with challenges that parents in the past never had to consider. On the one hand, we have an infinite amount of information and advice at our fingertips. Any questions that arise along our parenting journey can be researched instantly. We have unlimited access to books, articles, blogs, podcasts, studies, expert commentary, and Google search results. We're also able to connect with parents around the globe who can offer a range of support and perspective on any situation.

On the other hand, many of those benefits are accompanied by new landmines:

- We're overwhelmed with information, which can often lead to analysis paralysis or confusion.
- Not all of the information we view is credible. It's time-consuming and can be nearly impossible to differentiate between fact and fiction.
- Even when the information we find *is* verified, there's often an equally reliable study that offers a contradictory conclusion.

As a new parent who struggled to navigate all of my responsibilities at home and at work, I found the information I had at my disposal comforting on one level. I thought I could "educate" my way into work-life balance. If one resource or friend didn't hold the key to success, I'd just continue on to the next recommendation.

After years of failing to create a life that worked for my family and me, it occurred to me that this endless consumption of information was making matters worse. All it did was create a lack of confidence *within me*. It's not that the information wasn't credible. Sometimes it was, and other times it wasn't. The bigger issue was that I had no *filter* through which to assess all of the information and advice I encountered. Even the best advice fell short at times, simply because it wasn't applicable for *me* in that particular moment of my life.

We seldom realize that our most private thoughts and emotions are not actually our own. For we think in terms of languages and images which we did not invent, but which were given to us by our society. Alan W. Watts

Technology addiction

Technology addiction has become a pronounced issue in modern society. According to the Hazelden Betty Ford Foundation, "technology impacts the pleasure systems of the brain in ways similar to substances. It provides some of the same reward that alcohol and other drugs might: it can be a boredom buster, a social lubricant, and an escape from reality." And as we're discovering from the founders of social media conglomerates such as Facebook and Twitter, social media platforms in particular have been *specifically designed* to trigger that irresistible dopamine release that keeps us coming back for more.

Technology has become an addiction in many of our lives, but it can be a powerful tool if we learn how to manage it well. Technology allows more flexibility as we go about our day. Problems arise when we stop controlling our technology and allow it to control *us*. When we moderate our technology in intentional and strategic ways, it can make our lives easier.

We'll talk more about how you can maximize your use of technology and other tools in the second part of this book. In the meantime, two of my favorite resources for managing technology in general are *Digital Minimalism: Choosing a Focused Life in a Noisy World* by Cal Newport and *Indistractable: How to Control Your Attention and Choose Your Life* by Nir Eyal.

Echo chambers

Google, social media, and many other sources of information have become an echo chamber. Algorithms across all of our technology perpetuates confirmation bias, which means it's becoming more difficult to hear viewpoints that differ from our own. When our exposure to different experiences is so limited, it appears as though there are just a handful of "right" ways to parent. The reality is that there's an unlimited number of ways to be a good parent. When we're excluded from seeing the wide array of parenting choices that people make, we don't realize how unique and dynamic a working parent's experience really is. When we see the same limited values and behaviors reinforced, we may think that's the way it *must* be done. We feel pressured to fit in with our fellow parents. Furthermore, as the echo chambers intensify, we're less likely to follow our instincts and instead convince ourselves it's best to follow the herd.

Numbing out

We have an abundance of opportunities to numb out in our lives. Television, social media, food, alcohol, prescription medications, illicit drugs, obsessive analysis of our feelings, and overwork are all ways we try to limit pain or discomfort in our lives. It's hard to confront ourselves honestly. It's hard to acknowledge our weaknesses or bad habits or flaws. It's challenging to make a dedicated effort to overcome those flaws. Sometimes, it's even harder to embrace our inherent strengths and talents and to engage in habits that will integrate those unique gifts into our daily lives.

"Filling ourselves up" is very different than "numbing the pain." We rely far too much on the latter these days. We're feeling the effects of it, though. We suppress our emotions, problems, and needs by distracting ourselves with information, substances, social media, and other entertainment. Instead, we need to find ways to replenish our energy and well-being, which requires a personal process of trial and error.

Discrimination

I saved the most insidious obstacle for last. Racism, sexism, misogyny, misogynoir, xenophobia, and many other systems of oppression influence our experience as working parents every single day. Our society has been structured in many ways to prevent certain groups from obtaining power or equality, including women, Black, Indigenous, People of Color (BIPOC), religious groups, people with disabilities, and those in the LGBTQ+ community. These covert - and recently far too overt - biases have an impact on the stress levels of all working parents. There's an underlying power struggle playing out right now, and the outcome is uncertain. Too many working parents, on top of everything else they're dealing with, are forced to fight (often for their very lives) against patriarchy and white supremacy. While it would be nice to believe these factors don't exist, they do, and we need to honestly address how these biases impact us, both on individual and cultural levels.

In the last few years, we've seen women speak out against sexual harassment and abuse as part of the Me Too and Time's Up movements. African Americans continue to fight against police brutality, ongoing dehumanization efforts, excessive incarceration and systemic racism through the Black Lives Matter and other movements. Racial-ethnic minority and religious groups are fighting for equality as citizens in the United States and all around the world. The LGBTQ+ community just won their right to marry in the United States a few years ago, but they still fight against discrimination for equal civic rights in their everyday experiences.

We have a long way to go. Parents from all backgrounds are fighting for true equality. There's been resistance on the part of many men and white people around the world to release their death grip on that power and privilege to make room for a new world order that empowers oppressed groups. Understanding the true cost of these inequities, and overcoming them, is critical if we're ever going to fully support working parents in modern society.

————

Burnout is a complex phenomenon, as you can see. There's no single cause of the problem, and there's no one solution that's going to fix it. We wish it were as simple as integrating a new time management technique or self-care routine, but it's not. This problem has become widespread for *many* different reasons, occurring for each of us in different ways and to varying degrees. Overcoming burnout on a long-term basis is going to require deeply personal lifestyle changes. This book will help you make those lifestyle changes in a manageable way, taking into account the unique constraints, challenges, and goals of *your* life. It will require you to see the big picture of your unique life, rather than relying on generic solutions from others' lives.

That meltdown moment I had in the car with my husband kicked off a journey of personal discovery that continues to this day. I didn't know it yet, but in that moment, I acknowledged that I had fundamentally changed as a human being when I became a mom. I became willing to discover a new version of myself. I became willing to release my death-grip on my old perception of who I really was, deep down. I stopped fighting against the overwhelming change I was going through, and I started opening myself to the uncertainty of evolution. My instinct until then had been to hold on tight to everything that was familiar to me: my work style, my habits, my routines, my old values... my entire way of being. Living a fulfilling life as a working parent required trading the predictability of pain for the uncertainty of the future.

As I've been able to let go of older, more familiar versions of myself, I've given myself the space and freedom to discover who I truly am *today*. The longer I'm on this journey, the more I learn what I'm capable of as a mom, business owner, wife, daughter, sister, friend... as a *human being*. This process hasn't been easy. It's had its share of traps and challenges. It's opened up old wounds I'd prefer to leave in the past. But like the seasons, we have to leave old versions of ourselves in the past to grow into who we really are in this moment. That's where satisfaction as a working parent is accessible.

8

SELF-CARE CAN'T FIX THIS PROBLEM

The conversation around burnout has been gaining steam over the last few years. It seems that everyone is struggling with a lack of time, exhaustion, and this feeling that their life is all go-go-go. We're aware there's a problem. But the standard solutions aren't making a dent in the issue. In fact, the burnout epidemic seems to be getting worse.

We've all heard the advice to focus on self-care to combat those feelings of overwhelm, stress, and exhaustion. We have access to all of the information we could ever need as we search for solutions. Yet most of us are trapped in a vicious cycle of grinding through our endless to-do list until we collapse into bed at night. What are we missing?

The last few chapters outlined just a few of the personal, interpersonal, and cultural reasons why burnout persists for working parents. But there's one more reason that's so fundamental I thought it deserved a chapter on its own.

My experience with burnout isn't unique. I see the same toxic cycle happen every day for working parents. Juggling kids, a demanding career, our relationships, and managing a busy household, we push ourselves in all areas of our lives until we simply can't take on any more. Often, our bodies give out and we get physically ill. Other times we continue on autopilot while we check out of our lives mentally and emotionally. Life feels like a grind, but we power through.

Eventually, we turn to self-care out of necessity. We schedule a massage or an afternoon of golf or plan a date night with our spouse. Sometimes we even escape reality for a whole weekend away. After these short periods of rejuvenation, we return to our normal routine with renewed energy, ready to dive back into the chaos. Within weeks or even days, we're back in survival mode, and the whole process starts all over again.

Over the last few years, self-care has emerged as the key to overcoming burnout in many personal development circles. This well-intentioned advice is being distorted and may be perpetuating the burnout epidemic in our society.

When we're in survival mode, we search for anything that will offer immediate relief from our pain. Self-care can offer that much-needed relief. In that way, it's an important tool. If we're not careful though, we can get stuck in a pattern where we rely on self-care strategies as a Band-Aid solution to escape survival mode without addressing the *source* of our issues.

The short-term relief self-care offers can be used as an excuse to avoid examination of those lifestyle issues that caused the burnout in the first place. When we use self-care to dull the pain on a short-term basis, we convince ourselves all is well. We never get around to doing the deeper work of creating a *sustainable* lifestyle over the long term. Until we look beyond our symptoms, self-care strategies just camouflage what's happening under the surface.

Self-care is most effective in two situations: 1) when it's used as a tool to maintain an already healthy lifestyle, and 2) when it's used to energize you long enough for deeper self-reflection so you can integrate long-term changes. If you're using self-care strategies as a temporary solution to escape the depths of burnout, you're doomed to stay trapped in this toxic pattern.

———

SYSTEMS THEORY OFFERS A HOLISTIC APPROACH

I struggled for years to reconcile the tension I felt between the different roles I was playing in my life as a working parent. I felt like I was being pulled in a thousand different directions at all times. Whenever I turned my attention to one area of my life, everything else fell apart. Then I'd have to work overtime to get those other areas of my life back to baseline, which put me further behind everywhere else. I could never catch up.

As I explored the struggles working parents faced, I stumbled upon the key to creating a more sustainable lifestyle: Systems Theory. Systems Theory focuses on the arrangement of and relationship between parts that connect to become a whole. Systems exists in many different aspects of life, from nature to routines to relationships to engineering. A system is more than the sum of its parts, and changing one part impacts the others as well as the system itself.

Business Systems

I first learned about systems theory when I was a young paralegal in San Francisco. My ultimate job was to keep everything on track for the litigation cases to which I was assigned. I had to manage hundreds of different filing deadlines, exhibits, witnesses, client needs, and team dynamics. I had to know the various rules for every jurisdiction, every court, every judge, and every court clerk I engaged with on every case. I had to understand all of the different resources I had at my disposal in the firm so that I could utilize those resources as efficiently as possible.

There were thousands of details to manage, and it was my job to make sure it all aligned as efficiently as possible. I had to keep all of the parts of my cases working effectively on their own, but I also had to ensure they all worked *collectively* to achieve whatever goals the team had. My project management role evolved over the years, but every job I've ever had has required optimizing each independent part of a project in support of the larger whole.

Family Systems

Systems Theory has also played a significant role in the psychotherapy and coaching work I've done over the years. As a trained marriage and family therapist, we use systems thinking to understand the complex interactions of a family unit.

A family navigates complex interactions between different family members. Whenever one person does or says something as part of a family, it impacts the *whole* family. Patterns develop in the way we interact with the people we love. Those patterns can be healthy and functional, or unhealthy and dysfunctional. The goal in therapy is to identify the negative patterns that contribute to unhappiness in the family and then work to improve them. In personal development coaching, you can apply this same theory to different aspects of an individual's life.

Individual Systems

A couple of years ago, I also became trained in a therapeutic method called Internal Family Systems Theory. Internal Family Systems Theory, or IFS, explores the different parts of a person's psyche, and how those parts work to support the higher expression of *Self*. According to the IFS Theory developed by Dr. Richard Schwartz, we all have a complex group of sub-personality parts that make up our internal "system."

We can build a relationship with each of these independent parts by learning more about what they're each trying to accomplish. These little parts of our internal system are usually trying to protect us in some way. But no matter what's happening with each part, the *whole*, the *Self*, is always there and capable of being accessed. The parts can at times obscure the wisdom and authenticity of the Self, which is when we experience struggle or suffering. The IFS approach seeks to understand what those parts are trying to achieve in any given situation, so we can help them do their job in healthier and more effective ways.

 Growth is uncomfortable because you have never been here before, you've never been this version of you. So give yourself a little grace and breathe through it. Kristin Lohr

THE LAYERS OF OUR EXPERIENCE

As I synthesized my training in all different fields, I began to identify three overlapping systems that operate simultaneously for each of us. All of these systems have a huge impact on our experience of our daily lives. I've also come to think about these different systems in terms of MIND, BODY, and SOUL.

Life Management System
External | Mind

- Childcare
- Work responsibilities
- Home management
- Invisible Labor
- Routines and Systems

The Life Management System refers to all of the different obligations, responsibilities, activities, and pressures you face from *outside* sources. It's your *External System*. This external system often requires a lot of *logistical thinking* and *mental energy* to coordinate. This can include things like meeting work obligations, commitments you've made to your partner, parenting duties, or volunteer projects. They can also include things like household chores or the invisible labor that takes up your time and energy such as scheduling doctor appointments, paying bills, or planning a vacation. Your Life Management System always involves other people; they count on you to meet *their* needs within this system.

Emotional Intelligence System
Internal | Body

- Self-awareness
- Emotional regulation
- Relationships
- Motivation
- Empathy

The Emotional Intelligence System includes the thoughts, feelings, and sensations that are happening within your *body*. This is your *Internal System*. Your emotions, your mental and physical well-being, your habits, your energy levels, your relationships, and your boundaries are all a part of your Emotional Intelligence System. There are times when you may not be in tune with what's happening with this system.

This system can feel invisible, since it's not accountable to anyone besides you, and no one else can help you manage it. Your internal system can feel like it exists in the background, but it's a critical part of your experience as a working parent. Sometimes it seems prudent to ignore what's going on internally so you can focus on those external demands that *are* more visible. But if you ignore this system for too long your mental and emotional health starts to break down.

Personal Identity System
Foundational | Soul

- Core values
- Desires and goals
- Unique strengths
- Fears and triggers
- Higher purpose

The Personal Identity System refers to the values,

desires, goals, and unique qualities that make you.... *you*. This is your *Foundational System*. This is what makes your life worth living. This is your *soul in action*. These are the fundamental principles, beliefs, and personality traits that guide your life experience. Your personal identity influences your actions, ideas, perspectives, and insights. The more in touch you are with who you are on a foundational basis, the more you can utilize that deep inner awareness to create a life you love.

————

FLIP THE FOCUS

Most working parents who struggle with burnout are often living from the *outside in*. They get bombarded with *external* demands, and all of their time, energy, and focus go into meeting those external demands first and foremost. They are so focused on the Life Management System of their life that the Emotional Intelligence and Personal Identity Systems take a backseat. The problem with this approach is that the Emotional Intelligence and Personal Identity Systems are the source of *meaning* in our lives: our relationships, our ambitions, what gives us energy, how we feel about ourselves, what we're striving for, our very sense of *who we are*. When we neglect those systems, we lose control over our experience.

When working parents become consumed with external demands, their Emotional Intelligence System goes haywire under the surface. They feel stressed, depressed, disconnected, and anxious, but they're too busy to pinpoint why. They don't take the time to address their *emotional* or *interpersonal* needs, so their life spirals out of control.

When working parents lose touch with their Personal Identity System, they feel disconnected from their *current* core values: their deepest desires, how they've grown into parenthood, and what they want from their career now. They "feel different," but haven't had time to explore *how* their identity has changed, or how it guides their choices, behaviors, and beliefs in each moment.

Most working parents who struggle with burnout aren't managing *any* of these systems intentionally. They're too busy. Everything runs on auto-pilot (at best) or they become consumed with managing one emergency after another (at worst). Once we're in that situation, the only thing we know how to do is *react* to the most urgent fire without taking into account how our reaction will impact our systems *as a whole*.

Here's the truth we all intuitively know: blending all of these systems in a fulfilling way is the key to escaping burnout. But this isn't going to happen by accident. We need to reclaim control of our lives and manage each of these systems *deliberately*. The framework in Part 2 of this book will help you get a sense of all of the different elements of the systems that are operating in *your* life right now. You can also start to shine a light on some of the outdated beliefs, assumptions, behaviors, or parts of your identity that may not be serving you anymore.

CONSIDER THE BIG PICTURE OF YOUR LIFE

One of the most important things I've done to overcome burnout in my life is to integrate a practice of stepping *way* back to periodically evaluate the bigger picture of my life. I've learned I needed to identify and understand the *deeper root causes* of my struggles before I can ever hope to find an appropriate solution to those problems. Remember the story of the river babies at the beginning of this book? The Whole SELF Lifestyle is all about walking upstream to solve our problems, so we can leave behind the frantic struggle down river.

To me, being a working parent feels a lot like being an air traffic controller with different airplanes representing different aspects of my life:

- **Some airplanes are lined up on the runway, preparing to take off.** These are the plans I make ahead of time that keep my life running smoothly. This might look like having meal plans prepared for the week, establishing a comforting bedtime routine for my kids, or scheduling a relaxing massage.
- **Some airplanes are in motion, taxiing down the runway.** These are the projects or responsibilities that need my immediate attention. This might include a big work project I'm about to turn in, a client meeting I'm walking into, or a check-in on my mental health.
- **Some airplanes have just taken off and are flying out of my range of responsibility.** These are the items I am actively transitioning off my plate, either because they're complete, no longer necessary, or I'm outsourcing them to someone else. In my daily life, this looks like dropping my kids off at school, submitting a finished article to my editor, or wrapping up a workout.

- **Other airplanes are lined up in the air, ready to come in for a landing.** These are the most important areas of my life that require attention. If I don't get them on the ground safely and soon, bad things will happen. This includes making sure I'm regularly taking care of my health, spending quality time with my family, or engaging in my favorite activities purely for the joy of it.

As a working mom, I need to know where all of my "airplanes" are on a broad scale. But I also need to focus my attention on each airplane that's about to hit the runway in *that* moment. Working parenthood requires a constant process of *zooming out* to get a quick pulse on our life as a whole, and then *zooming back in* to focus all of our attention where it's needed most.

It wasn't until I became a working mom that I realized merely escaping my life for short bursts of time wasn't enough. I wanted to experience a more fulfilling life *overall*. As a result, I've had to adjust the way I manage my life to steer clear of burnout altogether. The key for me has been to leverage the extra energy I get from my ongoing self-care practice to improve the larger eco-system of my life as a *whole*. That's what leads to a satisfying lifestyle that *lasts*.

9

WHY SELF-AWARENESS IS CRITICAL

L
ast year I was recording an episode of the podcast I host and produce, the Working Parent Resource Podcast. In this particular episode, I analyzed some of the reasons why I personally have a hard time putting myself first even though I have all of the resources, advice, and inspiration I could ever need at my disposal. I asked the question: why hasn't *knowing* more led to a healthier and happier life as a working parent?

If you asked me in those early years of parenthood when I was struggling the most, here's what I would have said the problem was:

- I don't have enough time.
- My husband doesn't help out enough around the house.
- My kids are little and need me all the time.
- Society pressures me to be perfect.
- My coworkers are lazy.
- My boss doesn't care about my struggles.

- My clients are unreasonable.
- The world is too demanding.
- Being a working parent is just *hard*.

These are all reasons I wholeheartedly believed held me back from enjoying my life. If only these circumstances changed, I would be happy.

These are the topics that seem to drive the conversation around burnout for working parents today, too. Every mother's group I've ever been a part of is consumed with resolving the issues I listed above. Parents are desperate to find the book, strategy, or life hack that will reverse *those* problems. But nothing ever changes. More information isn't fixing our burnout problem. Why?

Surface-level symptoms reflect deeper issues that exist within us.

I just went through all of the internal, interpersonal, and cultural reasons why working parenthood is uniquely challenging. But there's even more to it. Everyone has a complex but unique set of reasons why we're unable to juggle the different areas of our lives in a way that feels *good* for us. And it has nothing to do with the reasons I just listed above. Those are all red herrings. Those are the reasons society wants you to *believe* you're unhappy, because those seem to be more manageable problems to solve.

Even more importantly, the people telling you these issues are the cause of your suffering are then primed to sell you something to fix it. If you don't have enough time, there's a productivity expert out there ready to sell you the perfect time management solution. If your boss is unreasonable, there's a career coach who can help you find a new position.

If your spouse isn't pulling their weight around the house, there's a marriage expert who will help you communicate more effectively with your partner. If your kids are falling behind on those all-important developmental milestones, there's a therapist who can give you behavior modification strategies to help your children meet those milestones.

To be sure, many of these professionals can have a positive impact on your life. These are important resources and people to rely on in times of suffering. But if you're struggling with *burnout*, you likely need a more comprehensive approach. Those singular solutions are too limited and don't take into account the *broader* and *inter-connected* context of your life.

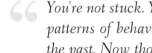 *You're not stuck. You're just committed to certain patterns of behavior because they helped you in the past. Now those behaviors have become more harmful than helpful.* Emily Marontian

BURNOUT IS A LIFESTYLE ISSUE

Here's an even bigger problem with believing those were the issues holding me back from living a happier life: *they all reside outside of me.* Whenever I believe my issues reside *outside* of me, three things happen:

1. I'm not motivated to do anything to fix it. I fall into "learned helplessness," a sense of powerlessness to change my own experience.
2. I adopt a victim mentality. I wait for *other* people to change and feel entitled to resentment and frustration until they do.
3. I get progressively more hopeless as

circumstances deteriorate over time. I feel like I've lost control over my own life, and have no idea how to get it back.

Even in cases where the *source* of our burnout does originate outside of us, such as in situations where things like poverty, abuse, discrimination, or a mental or physical disability are causing excessive adversity or stress, we still have to consider how *we* are going to adapt or respond to those sources of burnout. We all have different challenges and barriers to happiness. Some of those we can eliminate from our lives, and others we have to learn how to fight against or neutralize as much as possible. Cultivating an effective response to those situations still requires understanding the problem, the trauma we've experienced and continue to experience as a result, and the choices available to us in response. Ignoring, justifying, or simplifying those very real problems only intensifies our experience of it.

Your happiness, or fulfillment or contentment or joy or peace or whatever positive feeling you're striving for, comes down to *understanding yourself* enough to overcome the misunderstood or hidden reasons why your life isn't working for you right now. We're human beings, and there's often a lot going on under the surface that holds us back from being happy. Happiness is a by-product of living a meaningful life, whatever that means to each of us. If you're unhappy, there's no one *out there* who will be able to change that as well as *you* can.

―――――

SURFACE-LEVEL SYMPTOMS

We blame outside circumstances or people for the conditions in our life because it's what makes sense to us, given how we perceive the problem after a cursory look. No time? Just read a book to more effectively manage your time. Difficult boss? Find a new job. Your spouse isn't pulling their weight? Give them the silent treatment or an ultimatum. It's tempting to escape the discomfort of our problems as quickly as possible. So, our tendency is to get a quick understanding of the problem, and then move right into problem-solving mode. But until we understand the real issue, we're only addressing the *surface-level symptoms.*

We attempt to simplify our problems by focusing on the surface-level symptoms because we crave a quick fix. Especially as working parents, we don't have the time or energy for anything more complicated than that, right? We need it to go away immediately so we can get back to the demands of life.

The problem is, we've been buying into promises of a quick fix for complicated issues for years now. There's a quick fix offered in every article you read on social media. There's a quick fix provided in the advice you get from a fellow mom or dad friend who's in the trenches with you. There's a quick fix suggested in every class or workshop you take. But these quick fixes don't work. *None* of those writers, friends, or experts are familiar with the idiosyncrasies of *your* unique life. If you're reading this book, my guess is none of the quick fixes you've tried so far have succeeded in alleviating your burnout on a permanent basis.

Here's the secret no one wants you to know: *there is no quick fix.* Instead, there's a universe of *hidden-level issues* that will prevent you from creating the life you want until you identify, understand, and address them.

———

HIDDEN-LEVEL ISSUES

Hidden-level issues are much harder to see than surface-level symptoms, but they form the basis for our entire experience in life. Over the years, I've discovered just how deep that iceberg exists in my own life. Once I started exploring and resolving the root causes of my deeper issues, the surface-level symptoms either disappeared altogether or became much easier to manage.

Here are some examples of the types of *hidden-level issues* that prevented me from being happy for many decades, and still sometimes push me off course.

I'm a recovering codependent.

There was a long time in my life where my identity depended on making other people happy. When the people I loved were sad, I felt the need to fix it, and I would sacrifice anything in my own life to do that. When other people were struggling, I wholeheartedly believed it was my fault. When other people were self-destructing, I thought saving them was the only way to protect myself. If they weren't okay, by extension, I wasn't okay. My whole life revolved around understanding and changing *other* people's feelings. I was completely detached from my own.

I used to be afraid of confrontation.

Sacrificing my own needs in favor of maintaining the peace with people around me was a tradeoff I was willing to make in my early adult years. As long as I was agreeable and did what other people wanted me to do, I could avoid uncomfortable (or downright terrifying) confrontations.

I felt more secure when other people "needed" me.

As a child of divorce whose father lived on the other side of the country, I spent most of my life afraid of losing the people I loved. Ensuring that the people I loved needed me was almost like an insurance policy. If people needed me, they couldn't leave me, right? So I did everything in my power to make sure the people around me couldn't live without me. This underlying belief applied to my work relationships, friendships, and romantic relationships. Without realizing it, I sought out relationships with people who were struggling, and then I trapped them into needing me.

I thought giving everything of myself to someone else is what love *was*.

As a woman, the model I had of love was that I was supposed to give everything of myself. Then if the people around me loved me, they would do the same for me. I wasn't allowed to meet my own needs or ask for what I needed directly. That was "un-ladylike" or "selfish." Instead, I gave everything I had. Then I issued a guilt-trip if people didn't return the sentiment to the degree I needed. If others didn't contribute as much of themselves as I did, that was proof they didn't value me, which caused a whole other set of issues.

There are tiny humans who rely on me for survival.

As a mom, I have two little kids who literally rely on me for their survival. That responsibility feels overwhelming at

SARAH ARGENAL, MA, CPC

times, and it keeps me busy throughout my day. It can be hard to set that aside just so I can go and indulge in a bit of self-care, which is how it sounds in my head sometimes.

Focusing on other people allows me to avoid myself.

Sometimes, when something is going wrong in my own life, or I need to deal with a negative situation, it can feel more comfortable to turn off my mental and emotional turmoil and instead become the expert on someone else. If I'm focusing on someone else, I can critique and analyze and evaluate *them* and *their* life. I can leave my own problems behind for a while.

I got to feel superior.

My identity used to be built around the belief that I had my life totally together. I got a huge ego boost when I helped other people with their emotional issues or crises of the moment. I got to feel like a savior. I got to pretend that my life was perfect, because we weren't focusing on *my* life – we were focusing on *theirs*. I liked that feeling. It made me feel better about my own shortcomings. I also mistakenly believed it would protect me from critique or criticism from others. The same motivation drove my lifelong struggle with perfectionism and "playing small."

I used to think martyrdom was a virtue.

I used to equate martyrdom with self-worth. I linked my value to what I did to help other people. The more I suffered and sacrificed, the more virtuous a person I was. If I was drowning more than my co-workers, I was clearly the harder worker. If I was sacrificing myself for my family or friends, I got to throw my self-righteousness in their face whenever I was tired.

These are just a handful of the hidden-level issues that have persisted to varying degrees throughout my life. These complex, hidden beliefs used to control my choices, my behavior, my relationships, and as a result, my life experience. I've developed strategies to keep these natural inclinations in check over the years. It's gotten easier to replace those false beliefs with healthier ones, but these are all things I will always need to be aware of. They're ingrained in my hardwiring. If I never looked below the surface of my workaholic, people-pleasing, or perfectionist behaviors, I would still be trying to fix the *surface-level symptoms* without success. Finding lasting satisfaction in my life happened when I finally committed to investigating the *hidden-level issues* that triggered my *surface-level* behaviors and beliefs.

———

IT ALL COMES DOWN TO SELF-AWARENESS

Our world is noisy and relentless. It's increasingly abnormal in our modern world to operate from a steady source of self-possession. To be calm, confident, and unconcerned with the outside world's opinion of us is an act of defiance in our post-digital, social media age. But that's also what we all crave, deep down. We want to *know* ourselves, to *trust* ourselves, and to act from a reliable center of self. That all requires ***self-awareness***. None of the joy, confidence, and well-being we strive for is possible without it.

Addressing surface-level symptoms to overcome what's

causing pain in our lives might work for a little while, but when we face stress and adversity in our lives we fall back into our unconscious habits and entrenched patterns. We rely on coping skills that were established in early childhood or through traumatic experiences. These coping skills can be hard to identify, fix, and change over the long term since they're virtually invisible to us.

After twenty years of experience in the psychology field, one thing I know is that humans rarely keep doing something unless they're continuing to get some sort of payoff from it. That payoff could be measurable, like money, power, or status. Other times, that payoff could be more abstract, like love, approval from others, or a sense of approval or personal value. The question is: are your behaviors and beliefs generating a payoff that *benefits* you at this stage of your life? Or is the payoff actually *costing* more than it's worth?

As adults, we have access to resources and tools to improve our experiences that we didn't have when we were children. But it can be hard to overcome those old patterns and beliefs if we aren't aware of them. On the other hand, the more self-awareness we have in life:

- The more we can improve how we invest our time, energy, and attention.
- The more intentional and proactive we become.
- The more we understand *and own* our deepest values and desires.
- The more we reclaim control over our current identity.

It took me a long time to identify and explore all of the psychological dynamics that were happening under the surface in my life. Over the last two decades, I've worked with several different therapists and coaches. I've joined support groups. I've read thousands of books, studies, and articles on personal development, relationships, happiness, and psychology. I've learned valuable lessons from friends who are happy with various aspects of their lives. I've written in journals. I've meditated. I've taken retreats both domestically and abroad to explore my hidden patterns.

Discovering the variety and extent of issues that have held me back in life has taken time. It's not something that ever could have happened overnight. It has taken time to work through the grief, confusion, and clarity that comes with growth. There's no "easy button" for personal development. My life has improved progressively as I've committed to understanding myself on deeper and deeper levels over time. The process of self-discovery I've gone through has been intense at times, but I am so thankful I committed to my mental and emotional well-being.

Every day I face new struggles and challenges, and that's okay. There are also plenty of issues that I haven't eliminated completely from my life, but I've discovered healthier ways to manage them. Today I have the tools and a system of support to help me through difficult times. I'm not perfect. My life isn't perfect. But that's no longer the goal. I let go of perfection long ago. My only mission today is self-awareness.

_____

WE HAVE TO FIGHT FOR SELF-AWARENESS IN TODAY'S WORLD

Everything stems from self-awareness. Yet we are increasingly living in a society that *distracts* us from ourselves. It's tempting to think self-awareness is the equivalent of gath-

SARAH ARGENAL, MA, CPC

ering information, but that's not quite true. When we read a hundred books, or ask for advice from everyone around us, or listen to a dozen podcasts a week, what we're doing is downloading *other* people's self-awareness. Sometimes that can lead to our own growth. But if we don't know ourselves, if we don't have our own personal filter for that information, we take on all sorts of expectations that originate *outside* of us. We jump from one solution to another, searching in vain for that silver-bullet solution that will solve all of our problems and provide some relief. In the meantime, we sink deeper and deeper into hopelessness, anxiety, and burnout as other people's solutions don't work for us. We wonder what we're doing wrong.

The burnout epidemic dwells in a cultural obsession with meeting *external ideals* rather than developing a solid-state of *inner self-knowingness*. It can be hard to stick with the process of self-understanding in a society that values the opposite.

Contentment in life requires becoming more and more familiar with who *you* are, in a way that allows you to craft your life around those things that make you... *you*: your values, your strengths, your weaknesses, the people who encourage you to continue growing into your best self, finding work that fills you up and helps you contribute to the world in a meaningful way. There's a lot of advice out there to "be authentic" or "embrace your vulnerability." Expressing your *whole self* is impossible until you know what your whole self *is*.

104

10

THE NEW RULES OF WORKING PARENTHOOD

I like rules and structure. In my teen years, I paid attention to all of the different rules so I knew exactly how far I could bend those rules before I would get into trouble. I also worked in the legal field for twenty years. My specialty there was to understand the rules for every jurisdiction and judge to ensure our attorneys were in compliance. Rules have always provided a container within which I could get creative. Rules feel safe to me. For most of my life, I had no problem working within the rules imposed on me by society. In fact, mastering these rules allowed me to excel in my career and relationships in many ways. Society "approved" of me.

When I became a working mom, I realized the "rules" working parents were expected to follow cramped my style. They didn't feel right to me. At first, I didn't know what *did* feel right. But over the years, I've gotten a lot clearer about which rules work for me, and which ones I need to release. Now that my marriage, my kids' future, my career, my community, and my own health and well-being are on the line, it's clear to me I can't follow old rules developed long ago for a culture that no longer exists. I've learned it's critical that *I'm* the one writing the rules in my own life.

———

WHO ARE *YOU*... REALLY?

You don't have to change who you are to have a fulfilling life. You just have to get very *clear* about who you are and what you want in *this* stage of your life. Then commit to taking *action* to get to where you want to go. Part 2 of this book walks you through that process. It's designed to work in a world where you frequently feel overwhelmed, stretched thin, and like you have no time for even one more thing.

Working parenthood will test your limits. It will test your commitment to yourself and your family. It will test your motivation to find a system that works for you. As we discussed earlier, there are a number of personal and cultural elements that make it feel like the world is conspiring against us. It can be hard to find the strength to find solutions that work when you're sleep-deprived and drowning in responsibilities. You don't have time to experiment and learn through trial and error. You need answers... *now*.

As someone who specializes in the area of work-family conflict, I see it as one of my most important jobs to re-train people to look *within themselves* for insight and solutions. I encourage them to trust themselves, to embrace the unique nature of their conditions, rather than relying solely on the generic advice and opinions of others.

I've been referred to in the press as a "parenting expert," a "guru" and a "thought leader" over the years. I have a wide range of training in a variety of disciplines. But I couldn't possibly have all of the answers you need today. I don't know your life the way you do. I don't think you need more advice or instructions or strategies for success. Instead, I believe you need a *framework* you can use to discover those answers *for yourself*. So that's what I've developed for you.

 Shine so brightly you guide others out of the dark.
Anonymous

WORKING PARENTS ARE UNIQUE

Burnout isn't distinct to working parents. Many people, in all stages of life, struggle with burnout in modern society. But I specifically focus on the challenges working parents face for a few different reasons.

Working parents face unique challenges as they transition into parenthood.

This is especially true for parents who used to focus exclusively on their careers before having children. It's a complicated stage of life, and it naturally fosters new logistical and psychological hurdles. There are more constraints on your time, energy, and resources. You must navigate these new constraints while simultaneously coming to a new understanding of yourself, your relationships, your identity, and your life purpose. It's a lot to deal with all at once.

The future of our children is at stake.

We're failing the future generation right now. Every day we surrender to a frantic, burned-out existence, that's not just harming *our* well-being. We're also modeling that behavior for our kids. We need to teach our children that they can enjoy these precious years of *their* life by enjoying these precious years of *our* life.

The early years of a child's life are some of the most critical in determining who they'll become.

The fact that our kids' early years are also when working parents are stretched the most is an unnecessary tragedy. Working parents deserve support during this critical phase of their life and their kids' lives. The more help working parents get in the early years of their child's life, the more equipped they will be to positively influence the future generation.

Parents are desperate for change.

Burnout is on the rise. Despite everything we know, this problem is getting worse and shows no signs of diminishing unless we do something. My hope is that months of isolation with your family, while stressful, has given you that short period of breathing room you needed to start considering how you could craft a new lifestyle for yourself - one that *works*.

The good news is that we have what we need to overcome burnout. The reason working parents still struggle with burnout has nothing to do with a lack of knowledge or information. The reason working parents still struggle with burnout is because everyone is too tired to integrate *real* change into their lives. Working parents aren't lazy. They're overwhelmed and searching in vain for solutions that will provide *lasting* changes. They've tried everything they've been told hold the *secrets to success*, and it's all failed. Why keep trying? Better to just give up and power through the struggle.

Parents are the people in the best position to fix the negative aspects of our society.

It may sound idealistic, but I genuinely believe healthy, intentional, and nurturing parents can change the world through the connection, respect, and love they show their children. It's to everyone's benefit that we create a culture that gives working parents the space to do what they naturally strive to do: authentically love and support their kids. Showing up as our best selves at home and in the community has a positive ripple effect across society and across generations.

———

IT'S TIME FOR A REAL CHANGE

We're in the messy middle of a significant cultural shift. We realize that the "old" way of doing things hasn't worked, but we still haven't crystallized the "new" way of doing things either. We're at a breaking point as working parents. We've been burning the candle at both ends in a relentless digital age for nearly two decades now. We've received very little support and almost no acknowledgment of the pressure this lifestyle puts on working parents.

It's time to re-imagine a new approach to working parenthood. It's time to re-write the rules for ourselves. Our lives aren't going to become more manageable unless *we* start making different choices - one person, one family, and one community at a time.

In the next part of this book, we're going to focus on the four-step process I went through to escape survival mode. This is the exact process I've repeated over the years to refine and improve *every* area of my life. This is also the framework I've integrated into the work I do with individuals and groups over the years. I invite you to apply this framework to your life in whatever ways make the most meaningful impact in *your* life.

If it feels helpful, use it. If it feels inspiring, experiment with it. If it seems interesting, try it. If not... let it go, without guilt or fear of missing out.

Are you ready to start living a Whole SELF Lifestyle? Are you ready to discover who you are *today*, and what you're truly capable of? Are you ready to learn how to tune out the noise and start working from your own solid center? Let's do it.

PART II

11

THE PHILOSOPHY

So far, this book has been focused on my own experience as a working mom as I struggled to overcome burnout. And I've been largely successful. I have bad days like everyone else, but I can't remember the last time I've genuinely felt burned out. I've crafted a life that just *works better* for who I am now. I've also developed a system to prevent myself from getting to the point of no return. But that's *my* story. The specific strategies and steps I took to get there won't apply to you.

The rest of this book is about *your* story. It's about *your* journey out of burnout. The exercises you'll find in the coming chapters will help you reorient your life, so you can also start living from a place of *whole* self-awareness. I help break down this overwhelming, often intimidating process of discovering who you are *now*. You'll explore the different hidden-level issues that may be holding you back in life before you try to find solutions to those issues. You'll identify ways to improve the various systems that are operating in your life, while blending them all into one cohesive whole.

One of the biggest hurdles for working parents who are trying to create happier lives is the fact that it's hard to dive deep into self-discovery when you're in survival mode. It's hard to think about living your higher purpose or making sweeping changes in your life when you're stressed out or depleted or depressed or anxious. When you're in survival mode, you're focusing on *surviving* – and that's it.

Part of my work at the Argenal Institute is to avoid contributing to the noise out there. You don't need to know what worked for me or anyone else. You need to know what's going to work for *you*. This methodology will help you filter out all of the noise and create a life you love.

 Go *where there is no path and leave a trail.* Einstein

WHAT IS THE WHOLE SELF LIFESTYLE?

The Whole SELF Lifestyle is a *philosophy* as well as a practical *framework* to help working parents address the logistical and psychological challenges they face as they try to blend work, family, and life in general. It gives working parents a customized roadmap to escape survival mode on their own terms. We'll cover the philosophy of the Whole SELF Lifestyle in this chapter, and then move on to how the framework breaks down in the next chapter.

The Philosophy

The Whole SELF Lifestyle philosophy offers an alternative to the hustle-and-grind culture that's taking over our society right now. It encourages dedicated professionals to make the most of their lives without sacrificing what matters most to them. This approach is about creating a lifestyle that works for *you*, based on your unique strengths, needs, desires, circumstances, and goals. And as a busy working parent, you need a flexible system that can work within the various constraints of your life.

First, it's essential to understand the big picture of your life. Then from there, you'll be in a better position to target the specific areas that need attention. Once you have a deeper understanding of yourself and your life as a whole, you can make more effective choices based on what you need in each moment. The primary goal of the Whole SELF Lifestyle process is to get you immediate relief while simultaneously pursuing long-term growth in all areas of your life.

———

THE 3 PILLARS OF THE WHOLE SELF LIFESTYLE

There are three main components of the Whole SELF Lifestyle that all work together simultaneously.

Pillar #1: Whole

We, as human beings, are meant to feel *whole*. As working parents, we're always fielding demands and pressure from the outside world. Being in reaction mode to all of these different areas of our lives can make us feel scattered, stretched thin, depleted, and resentful. I often hear working parents using these phrases to describe their experience trying to stay on top of everything they manage on a day-to-day basis:

- *I don't have enough time.*
- *Balance isn't possible.*
- *I never have enough energy.*
- *I'm drowning.*
- *I can't keep up.*
- *I'm failing at everything.*
- *My to-do list is a mile long.*
- *I'll take care of myself when things slow down.*

Many of the obligations we face are indeed important. We can't just ignore them. But others could potentially be put on the back burner for a while. Others really could be dismissed indefinitely without any major consequences. But until you take the time to critically evaluate everything that's coming at you from the outside world, it will be difficult to make informed decisions about your life. The Whole SELF Lifestyle helps you integrate all of the different areas of your life into one functioning whole.

Pillar #2: Self

Becoming a parent has a way of shattering everything we thought we knew about ourselves. Our identity goes through a significant transformation, a deepening. We inevitably surrender old parts of ourselves. We take on new roles in our relationships and our lives. We start to understand ourselves in different ways. We face all sorts of new circumstances, which require new skills and perspectives to adapt to. We try to blend who we used to be with who we are becoming. But so many working parents today are too busy to explore this shifting identity in any useful way. I often hear working parents use phrases like:

- *I don't know who I am anymore.*
- *I've lost myself.*
- *I miss who I used to be.*
- *I don't know what to do.*
- *I feel so guilty.*
- *I'm unhappy.*
- *There has to be more to life than this.*

When we're not clear about our inner world, we become increasingly persuaded by outside influences. We rely on experts and "gurus" and opinions of friends and family. This reliance on external sources for wisdom leads to a loss of confidence to do what's best for ourselves, our families, and our future. Our sense of self, as a result, isn't understood deeply enough to guide our choices, behavior, or beliefs in a meaningful way. We're living from the outside in, which is backward. When this happens, it's easy to find ourselves living out other people's agendas and values rather than our own. This is what makes life as a working parent feel like a grind, an endless loop of non-stop responsibilities. The Whole SELF Lifestyle helps you go through a process of self-discovery that honors the different parts of who *you* are so you can approach every situation you encounter with a solid sense of *self*. It gives you confidence that the choices you make are right for *you*.

Pillar #3: Lifestyle

The third part of this philosophy is all about establishing a healthy *lifestyle*. Creating a fulfilling life is not a destination. It's not an outcome. It's not something to achieve. It's a *practice*. It's an ongoing discipline. It's a way of being in the world. It will fluctuate. Some days you'll be better at it than others. As long as you get clear about who you are and keep your intentions top of mind, the demands of daily life won't pull you off track as easily. And when you *do* get pulled off track, you'll know how to course-correct quickly. The Whole SELF Lifestyle helps you replace the constant searching for answers outside of yourself with a *reliable* and *repeatable* process that will support you in discovering the right answers for you in each season of your life.

The 3 pillars of the Whole SELF Lifestyle remind us to stay grounded within our *whole self* as we move through the chaos that comes with working parenthood. It helps us explore our old, unconscious patterns of behavior, understand those patterns on a deeper level, and make healthier choices going forward. It's a way to up-level the baseline of our thoughts, beliefs, perspectives, decisions, behaviors, and experiences. Over time, we gradually improve our lives in every area.

PUTTING THE WHOLE SELF LIFESTYLE INTO PRACTICE

The next four chapters will explore the Whole SELF Lifestyle *framework*, which breaks down the philosophy into four distinct action-oriented steps. You'll find a series of self-reflection questions, exercises, and prompts to help you understand yourself and the circumstances of your life on a deeper level. These are questions you can start answering one by one today. It doesn't require a huge life change. You are encouraged to begin with small steps to avoid overwhelm. The key is that you're looking at the big picture of your life. From there, you can make strategic choices about all areas of your life.

12

THE FRAMEWORK

The Whole SELF Lifestyle framework helps busy working parents break the abstract philosophy down into concrete steps in their own lives. This 4-step framework offers a holistic guide to help you understand not only the surface-level symptoms you're feeling in your life, but also the *real* source of your struggles within the context of a more extensive system.

By breaking things down and starting from where you are now, you're able to make manageable but immediate changes that will give you back the time, energy, and focus you need to continue to make more changes over time. These small changes will impact the broader ecosystem of your entire life. Instead of scrambling to find the next "silver bullet" solution to your problems, or numbing out because you can't manage your life anymore, you'll start crafting the lifestyle that works for *you*, in *this* season of your life. It's all done in a strategic way that provides some much-needed clarity and peace now, but also keeps in mind the longer-term vision you have for your life.

I use the acronym S.E.L.F. to break down the Whole SELF Lifestyle philosophy into a practical four-step process.

STEP 1: (S) SYSTEM INVENTORY

Our lives are made up of a complex series of internal and external systems that operate simultaneously. The more efficient each part of these systems is, and the more they're designed to operate in congruence with each other, the happier and healthier we feel in our lives – the more *whole* we are. The first step of the Whole SELF Lifestyle framework is to *complete an inventory* of the different systems that are operating in your unique life so you can use *that* reality as a starting point for lasting change.

STEP 2: (E) EVALUATE

Once you have identified the different systems that are currently active in your life, it's time to *evaluate* each one to see what's working for you and what isn't. You also analyze how all of the systems are working together in your life. Then you decide what you want your life to look like – your ideal. Once you've analyzed these systems, and how things are working together, then you can identify what needs to happen to get from where you currently are to where you want to go.

STEP 3: (L) LIST OF SOLUTIONS

The first two steps of the Whole SELF Lifestyle framework provide clarity and a roadmap for change. Now you're in a position to *brainstorm the action steps* that will improve different areas of your life. This is when it's helpful to do research, listen to podcasts, read books, get advice, etc. Then you can make an educated decision about your next steps. Doing the first two steps of this framework limits overwhelm and bright shiny object syndrome, and allows you to focus on the best next steps for you in this moment of your life.

STEP 4: (F) FAMILIARIZE

In this final step, you *implement* and *experiment*. You try out different action steps you brainstormed in the last step. You decide what really works for you, your family, your career, and your life – and what doesn't. You discard what doesn't work, and you repeat what does work so it becomes a new habit in your life. You refine and evolve based on what you learn. Over time, you familiarize yourself with new ways of being in the world, new habits, new routines, and a more satisfying lifestyle that's centered around your *whole self.*

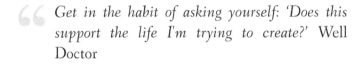

Get in the habit of asking yourself: 'Does this support the life I'm trying to create?' Well Doctor

This action-oriented process allows you to start big and broad to get a big-picture perspective of your life. Then once you have a clear high-level view of what's happening in your life, you can make informed decisions to drill down into the areas of your life that need the most attention. The result will be long-term changes based on a clear understanding of who you are now, what you need, what you want, and the best way forward in your *current* circumstances.

Remember the air traffic controller? To do their job effectively, they need to regularly keep the big picture in mind, while also zeroing in on each plane that needs the most attention in each moment. It's time to put on the "air traffic controller" hat in *your* life.

We're going to expand your vantage point so that you can make more informed choices. Knowing where to place your time, energy, and attention will alleviate the guilt, second-guessing, and shiny object syndrome that plagues many working parents. When you make a choice, *any* choice, you'll know exactly why. You'll have a broader perspective, and you'll understand how changes in one area of your life might impact all of the others because you've consciously thought it through.

Once you've gone through the Whole SELF Lifestyle framework once, you can use it as a tool over and over again in your life. You can repeat these steps whenever you're feeling burned out, or when a significant life shift happens, or if you're just craving an upgrade in the quality of your life. You can apply this methodology to any situation in your life. You can also use this framework on a broad basis to examine every area of your life, or you can zoom in on trouble areas to get more immediate and specific relief as needed.

Self-discovery happens, and can *only* happen, if you go through *all four* of these steps. Most people today spend all of their time in the third step, ignoring all of the other stages of the growth process. Accumulating information indiscriminately and failing to put anything into action contributes to those feelings of overwhelm, failure, and guilt since you're just consuming information without any strategy, direction, or purpose to put it into practice.

———

HOW TO APPLY THIS FRAMEWORK

Go through the questions in the next four chapters to explore the systems that are currently consuming *your* time, energy, and attention. These questions are meant to be thorough, but they're certainly not exhaustive. There will be aspects of your life that should be addressed even if they don't pop up in this inventory. Allow yourself to continue to explore and deviate and dig further based on what's coming up for you. This is a personal process, and if these questions either don't apply to you, or if there's anything missing.... go with what's true for *you*. Think of this as a jumping-off point, and then follow your own path wherever it takes you.

You may be tempted to ignore the next few chapters. It may seem overwhelming, or just too much to dive into right now. It's okay to gloss over the questions now, finish the book, and then come back to dive into the exercises later. But know that the *real* transformation you're looking for comes from answering these questions, and then integrating the insight you gain into your daily life. You don't have to do it all in one sitting (please, don't!). Take your time. Do it at your own pace. But do follow these general guidelines to get the most out of this process (and your life).

1. **Answer each question honestly.** The more honest you are in your responses, the more impact you'll feel. Remember, no one else will see your answers besides you (unless you want them to), so get *real*.
2. **Avoid self-judgment.** Don't assign a label of "good" or "bad" to any of your answers. Think of yourself as a neutral observer as you answer these questions.
3. **Be brief.** Don't feel compelled to write several pages per answer (unless you want to!). The goal

here is to provide clarity for yourself in a variety of areas in your life. Your answers can start with a short overview based on what immediately comes to mind for you. Give yourself permission to touch on the most important parts of each answer. A few sentences will do. When something striking arises, feel free to get more in-depth on those questions, if you're inspired to do so.

4. **Give yourself time.** Don't feel like you have to answer all of these questions in one sitting. Focus on a handful of questions at a time, and then give yourself a break. Self-reflection can be mentally and emotionally draining, and there's no need to rush through this process. Remember, this is a *lifestyle*, not a quick fix. There will also probably be times when you're in the "flow" and are motivated to keep going. That's okay too! Just follow your instincts without judgment, and you'll get through it at the perfect time.

5. **Be compassionate with yourself.** The tendency when you complete these exercises is to focus on everything that needs to be "fixed." But don't forget to identify what you do *well* too! We are all a mix of strengths and weaknesses. Be honest but be fair to yourself also. Avoid the temptation to be overly critical.

6. **Allow your responses to change.** You are a living, breathing human. Your life circumstances are changing moment to moment. The lessons you learn accumulate over time, which will change your perspective and needs. Use that information to refresh your responses as needed.

As I write this book, most of the world is under a stay-at-home lockdown order to avoid spreading the coronavirus disease. The answers you come up with in that situation are going to vary greatly from the responses that come up when life is relatively normal. That's okay. Let this be a living document that reflects wherever you are *today*.

———

BONUS LIBRARY

I've prepared a handful of bonus materials to help you dive deeper into the following exercises. You can access these bonus materials in **The Whole SELF Lifestyle Bonus Library** here: www.wholeselflifestyle.com/working-parents/bonus-library.

———

COMPANION WORKBOOK

Or if you're someone who loves working with a real pen and paper, we also have a physical workbook version of these exercises. **The Whole SELF Lifestyle for Working Parents Companion Workbook** is available here: www.wholeselflifestyle.com/working-parents/companion-workbook.

13

STEP 1: (S) SYSTEM INVENTORY

The first step of the Whole SELF Lifestyle framework is "**S**," for **System Inventory**. The System Inventory is a critical part of the Whole SELF Lifestyle. Without a clear understanding of all of the different micro-systems that make up your life, you'll continue to feel like you're *reacting* to your life. This process of identifying the details of the systems in your life will set the foundation for the rest of our work.

Answer these questions as they apply to you *today*. You may feel tempted to skip the questions that don't seem "relevant" or that aren't causing you the most difficulty right now. *Avoid the temptation to skip any questions.* We often discover hidden treasures in the least likely places. It's also important to get the broadest perspective possible. You may be surprised at what comes up for you or how different areas of your life are connected when you explore all of the nooks and crannies of your life.

> *It's the small habits. It's how you spend your mornings. How you talk to yourself. What you read. What you watch. Who you share your energy with. Who has access to you. That will change your life.* Michael Tonge

SELF-INQUIRY QUESTIONS

*You can access the **System Inventory Snapshot** in the **Bonus Library** at www.wholeselflifestyle.com/working-parents/bonus-library.*

———

LIFE MANAGEMENT SYSTEM
EXTERNAL | MIND

This section relates to all of the *external*, *logistical* aspects of your life as a working parent.

Family

- Who is in your immediate, nuclear family (spouse/partner, kids, pets)?
- Who is in your extended family (parents, grandparents, siblings, aunts, uncles, cousins, in-laws, etc.)?

Career and Purpose

- What is the role of your career in your life right now?

- What is your primary job or source of income?
- Do you have any side projects that you're working on? If so, what does that entail?
- Are you dedicating your time to any volunteer pursuits? Please describe.
- What other passions or hobbies are you currently focused on?
- Are there any other contributions you're making in your career or to fulfill a deeper purpose in your life?
- What are your professional goals for the future? One year from now? Five years from now? Ten years from now?

Household Management

- How does the role of household management factor into your life right now?
- How do you feel about the current state of your home environment?
- How organized are you, in general?
- How do household chores currently get done in your home?
- How do you maintain a functional and organized space? Who else is involved in maintaining your home?

Systems and Processes

- Who handles your family schedule?
- How do you keep your work, family, and other obligations organized? Do you have a to-do list? Family Calendar?

- How do you organize your mail and paperwork? What happens to those items when they come in?
- How do you manage your finances and bills? Do you have a budgeting system?
- What's your system for organizing, signing, and returning school paperwork?
- How do you maintain important papers (wills, marriage licenses, birth certificates, marriage certificates, etc.)?
- How do you plan for and prepare meals? Breakfast? Lunch? Dinner? Snacks? Weekdays? Weekends?
- Who is currently responsible for carpool and supervising after-school activities?
- Who handles errands in your home?

Childcare

- Who is responsible for feeding your kids? Breakfast? Lunch? Dinner? Snacks? Weekday? Weekend?
- Who handles getting the kids dressed every day?
- How do you manage the supervision of your children?
- How do you feel about your kids' education right now?
- Who is involved in the cognitive, moral, and social and emotional development of your family?

Mental Load

- How does vacation research generally happen in your family?
- How are doctor's appointments scheduled? For the kids? For you? For your partner?
- How are school supplies prepared each day? Packing backpacks, extra clothes, diapers, lunch, bottles, etc.?
- How do you hire and supervise other workers in your home (nannies, housekeepers, assistants, dog walkers, etc.)?
- Who takes care of your pets if you have any? What does that entail?
- How are major life transitions handled in your family (big moves, job changes, new baby, new school years, etc.)?
- How do you handle 401(k), life insurance, car insurance management? Who is generally responsible for this?
- What other activities and responsibilities do you think about regularly that weren't listed?

———

The ***Family Management Plan*** in the ***Bonus Library*** *will help you identify the full range of household management and invisible labor required in your daily life. Access it here now: www.wholeselflifestyle.com/working-parents/bonus-library.*

———

Routines

- How do you manage your morning routine right now?
- What's involved in your evening routine?
- How do you manage the kids' school or daycare schedules right now?
- What is involved in your current work schedule and demands? Do you have any excessive stress related to work right now? Describe.
- How do you fit exercise into your schedule right now? What fitness activities do you enjoy doing most?
- What kind of spiritual practice do you integrate into your day? Meditations, prayer, church, journaling?

Family, Friends, and Social Events

- How much time do you need alone to re-charge?
- How much time do you need with others to re-charge?
- How do you integrate time to re-charge into your daily routine right now?
- How do you decide when to spend time with your spouse right now? What does that time together usually include?
- When do you usually get to spend quality time with your close friends? What does that typically look like for you?
- How do you decide which social activities to commit to?

Organization

- Digital: How do you organize your digital life (mobile device, computer, etc.)?
- Time: How do you make decisions about your time?
- Physical: How do you stay organized at home? At work? In your car? In other areas of your life?

What did I miss?

- What other areas are you focusing on that I didn't list above?
- What other obligations do you have right now?
- What other systems or routines are a big part of your life?

EMOTIONAL INTELLIGENCE SYSTEM
INTERNAL | BODY

This section relates to all of the ***internal***, ***psychological***, and ***relational*** aspects of your life as a working parent.

Self-Awareness

- How often do you do self-development work?
- How often do you find yourself feeling disconnected from who you are, deep down?
- How well do you feel you know yourself right now?

- How do you stay in tune with yourself generally throughout the day?
- Do you have a mindfulness practice right now? If so, what does that involve?

Physical Health

- How do you support your physical health?
- How does your physical health impact your experience of the world?
- What do you need to be at your best physically?

Mental Health

- How do you support your mental health?
- How does your mental health impact your experience of the world?
- What do you need to do to be at your healthiest, mentally?

Emotional Health

- How do you support your emotional health?
- How does your emotional health impact your experience of the world?
- What do you need to be at your best emotionally?

Motivation

- When do you feel most motivated?
- What personal goals do you have for yourself right now?

- What professional goals do you have for yourself right now?
- What do you feel your eternal life purpose is?
- How do you integrate habits into your life to ensure you get what you want?
- Do you have any bad habits in your life you'd like to change? How would you like those habits to be different?

Energy

- Where do you get your energy?
- What *gives* you energy? What activities? Which people?
- What *depletes* your energy? Which activities? Which people?
- When are you usually the most focused? What time of day? What are the circumstances?
- When do you usually go into "auto-pilot" mode, when you're in motion, but not particularly conscious about what you're doing?
- What role does recreation and hobbies play in your life?
- What hobbies did you enjoy before parenthood?
- Which of those hobbies do you miss? Which would you like to integrate into your life today?
- What makes you feel *complete*?
- When do you feel most in the "flow" (entirely focused on what you're doing, with no distractions)?
- What do you wish you had more time to do?
- What activities do you most enjoy now?

- If time wasn't a factor, what would you do more of?
- What activities are a "part" of you? Which can't you do without?
- What do you do purely for *fun*?

Marriage and Committed Partnerships

- What is the role of marriage or committed partnerships in your life right now?
- What were the qualities that attracted you to your partner when you first met them?
- What are your favorite qualities about your partner now?
- Who were your biggest relationship influences throughout your life?
- Who were your partner's biggest relationship influences?
- What are your biggest strengths as a couple?
- How do you and your partner handle conflict?
- What is *your* primary role in your marriage?
- Your *partner's* primary role in your marriage?
- How do you handle co-parenting with your partner?
- What do you do for fun together?
- How do you support each other as individuals?
- How do you divide household management?
- How do you divide the invisible labor?
- What are you *most* satisfied with in your relationship right now?
- What are you *least* satisfied with in your relationship right now?
- How do you spend your free time together?

- If you're not currently in a committed relationship, what qualities are you looking for in a partner? Are you in a place where you are looking for a partner at all right now? If not, what are you focused on instead?

Relationship with Your Kids

- What is *your* role as a parent?
- What is your *partner's* role as a parent? How are they different from each other?
- What were the biggest parenting influences from your childhood?
- What were your partner's biggest parenting influences from their childhood?
- How are your kids unique as people? What are their most defining traits?
- What are your biggest strengths as a parent?
- What are your partner's biggest strengths as a parent?
- How do you connect best with your kids?
- How do you integrate spending quality time together as a family into your week?
- How do you adapt to new ages, stages, and changes as your kids grow?
- How do you deal with challenging behaviors?
- What's most important to you as a parent? What is your primary purpose as a parent, if you had to choose one?

Extended Family

- Who is in your family of origin? Who did you grow up with?
- Parents
- Siblings
- Blended family members
- What is the role of extended family in your life?
- Do you still have grandparents in your life?
- Who are the aunts, uncles, and cousins in your life?
- What do each of these people contribute to your life?
- Do you have any struggles or issues with any of these people?

In-Laws and Co-Parents

- Who are your parents-in-law?
- Who are your siblings-in-law?
- Blended in-law family members, if any?
- Do you have any ex-partners or co-parents in your life? Who are they?
- Do you have any adoptive family members?
- Who else is in your family? Did I miss anyone? Add them here.
- What do each of these people contribute to your life?
- Do you have any struggles or issues with any of these people?

Friendships and Community

- What is the role of friendships in your life?

- Who are your closest friends? What do you love most about them?
- Who are your oldest friends? How have you stayed in each other's lives all these years?
- Who are your professional friends?
- Who are your neighbors?
- Who are your more distant acquaintances?
- What other community contacts do you have in your life right now?
- Are there any relationships that are causing you stress?

Empathy and Compassion

- How do you escape the natural limits of your own perspective? How do you open yourself to what other people are experiencing?
- How are you able to see things from another's point of view?
- Do you feel comfortable sitting in silence with someone who is struggling?
- How do you best provide support to your loved ones who need it?
- Do you offer *empathy* (bringing up your own emotions to connect with someone else) or *sympathy* (feeling a sense of compassion for someone else who is struggling with something you haven't felt)?
- Are you able to accept others for who they are without trying to change them?
- How do you cope with other people's struggles and big emotions?

SARAH ARGENAL, MA, CPC

PERSONAL IDENTITY SYSTEM
FOUNDATIONAL | SOUL

This section relates to all of the *foundational*, *non-negotiable* aspects of your life as a working parent.

Identity

- What is your overall understanding of *who you are?*
- How has your view of yourself changed over time?
- How can you integrate a regular practice into your life to refresh your view of yourself over time?
- What are some of the most prominent defining characteristics of your identity today? What makes you... *you?* Today?

Values

- What are your *Current Values?* What's most important to you on a fundamental level right now?
- What are your *Aspirational Values?* What are you striving for in your life?
- What are your biggest *Priorities* for this season in your life? Choose no more than three.
- What actions can you take to further your values in your day-to-day life?

———

Check out the **Values & Priorities Profile** *exercise in the* **Bonus Library** *to help with this section. You can access it here now:* www.wholeselflifestyle.com/working-parents/ bonus-library.

———

Core Beliefs

- What are some of the most notable stories you heard as a child?
- What is your perspective on the world, based on your life experience?
- What do you *believe* to be true?
- When is the first time you remember believing this? Describe the situation.
- How does this belief show up in your life today?
- What do you get out of believing this now? What's the payoff for you?
- Are you making any assumptions that may not be true?
- What do you *know* for sure?
- What drives you? What are you confident about in your life today?

Accomplishments

- Which accomplishments (personal or professional) are you most proud of?
- What allowed you to achieve those things?

- What do you believe was the key to your being able to achieve those things?
- How do you feel about claiming credit or pride in your accomplishments? How does it feel to you?

Personality Traits

- What are some of your best personality traits?
- Which personality traits would you like to develop, improve, or change?
- What's the flip side of that personality trait? How can you express that trait in a healthier way?

Life Vision

- What did you want your life to look like when you were younger?
- What's the most recent life vision you had for yourself?
- Take a breath. Get focused on who you are *now*. What would you like your life to look like in one year? In three years? In ten years?
- How has your life vision changed since the last time you've asked yourself this question? How have *you* changed?
- What are you currently striving for in each of these areas of your life: Career and purpose, Family, Self?

Regrets

- Do you have any regrets in your life? If so, what's your biggest regret in your life so far?

- Have you been able to forgive yourself for this regret? If not, why not?
- Have you been able to forgive anyone else who may have been involved? If not, why not?
- What have you learned from these experiences that you have (or can) integrate into future experiences?
- Have you been able to move on from these regrets in your life, or do they hold you back today?
- If they're still holding you back, how does that look in your day to day life?

Triggers

- What are some of your biggest triggers?
- Negative Triggers: What triggers you to behave in ways you *don't* want to?
- Positive Triggers: What helps you behave in ways you *want* to?
- Are there any experiences or stories that others share that create difficulty for you?
- What reminds you of negative past experiences?
- What motivates you to act when you don't want to?

Fears and Insecurities

- What are some of your biggest fears? What are you most afraid of today?
- Do you notice any particular insecurities about yourself? What do you wish you could hide from others?

- How do those fears or insecurities currently hold you back from living the type of life you want?
- Do you know where these fears or insecurities originated?

Perceived Strengths

- What do you believe are your biggest strengths today? In what ways are you *awesome*?
- How did you develop those strengths?
- How can you build on these strengths in your life?
- How do these strengths contribute to your life?

Perceived Weaknesses

- What do you believe are your most limiting weaknesses right now?
- What do you struggle with the most?
- How do you feel about these weaknesses? Are you actively trying to improve them, or do you accept them?
- Do you *want* to improve these weaknesses?

Treasured Moments

- What are your most treasured moments to this day?
- What do those moments mean to you? How do they contribute to your overall understanding of yourself?
- Are you able to share these moments with others in your life? Why or why not?

- What types of circumstances led to these treasured moments?
- Do you see a pattern among your most treasured moments (i.e., what do you look back on in your life with the most fondness and love)?
- Are you able to craft a life that will improve your chances of collecting *more* treasured moments?
- When you look back on your life, what do you believe will be the moments you remember most?

Spirituality and Connection

- What is the role of spirituality in your life today?
- Do you have a religious or spiritual practice (church, meditation, retreats, journaling, etc.)?
- What are your most effective self-reflection practices?
- How do you connect with society on a larger scale? How do you get out of your head and develop meaning in your life?
- How do you make time to connect to your higher power, or to something greater than yourself (if you're not spiritual)?

NEXT STEPS

Whew! You did it! I know that was a lot of questions. I hope you took some time between the questions to gather your energy and to reflect as you needed to.

Now you have some real, *current* data to work with. In the next chapter, we're going to do some analysis to identify where you can make some changes and start to enjoy this working parenthood journey.

––––––

BONUS RECAP

You can find these bonus materials in our **Bonus Library** at: www.wholeselflifestyle.com/working-parents/bonus-library.

- **System Inventory Snapshot**
- **Family Management Plan**
- **Values & Priorities Profile**

Also, remember you can get the **Companion Workbook** here as well: www.wholeselflifestyle.com/working-parents/companion-workbook.

14

STEP 2: (E) EVALUATE

The second step of the Whole SELF Lifestyle framework is "**E**," for **Evaluate**.

Now that you have a clear idea of the different micro-systems that are operating in your life right now, it's time to analyze those systems, first independently and then as a whole, to determine what's working well and what could be working better. Answer these questions for each system to identify the areas where you can focus your time and energy to make the most intentional changes in your life.

You don't need to know how you'll make these changes yet. That'll come in the next step. For now, you're just pinpointing the things that you would like to change. Try not to judge or edit your answers to these questions. Make a laundry list of the things that you *like* about this area of your life, and the things you want to *improve* or work on. I know it can seem impossible to fix whatever struggles you're facing in these areas, but it's worth assessing the different areas of your life without getting pulled immediately into problem-solving mode.

You also don't have to look at your entire life all at once. That can feel overwhelming, especially in the beginning. You can start by focusing on just one area of your life. Some people start with the area that's causing them the most stress, where they need immediate relief. Other people start with an area that's meaningful for them, such as their relationship with their kids or spouse. Other people focus on an area that will make it easier to work on the *other* areas, like managing their energy or mental health.

Once you have all of the different areas of your life laid out in front of you from the first step, it's a lot easier to make some educated decisions about where to drill down to focus your efforts.

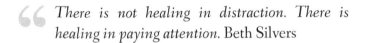 *There is not healing in distraction. There is healing in paying attention.* Beth Silvers

EVALUATE

*You can access the **Evaluate Checklist** in the **Bonus Library** at: www.wholeselflifestyle.com/working-parents/ bonus-library.*

LIFE MANAGEMENT SYSTEM
EXTERNAL | MIND

Out of all of the **Life Management** areas you identified in the last chapter, which 3 systems feel *least* satisfying for you right now? Which areas do you want to prioritize first? List them in order of priority.

1.

2.

3.

If you had to focus on *one* area to improve first, which of these systems do you feel compelled to work on first? This can be the area you identified as being least satisfying to you, but it may also be an area that you've been wanting to improve for a while, or an area you think will improve the others. Which area would you like to focus on first?

LIFE MANAGEMENT SYSTEM: *List your **top** priority here for easy reference.*

EMOTIONAL INTELLIGENCE SYSTEM
INTERNAL | BODY

Out of all of the **Emotional Intelligence** areas you identified in the last chapter, which 3 systems feel *least* satisfying for you right now? Which areas do you want to prioritize in our work now? List them in order of priority.

1.

2.

3.

If you had to focus on *one* area to improve first, which of these systems do you feel compelled to work on first? This can be the area you identified as being least satisfying to you, but it may also be an area that you've been wanting to improve for a while, or an area you think will improve the others. Which area would you like to focus on first?

———

EMOTIONAL INTELLIGENCE SYSTEM: *List your* ***top*** *priority here for easy reference.*

———

PERSONAL IDENTITY SYSTEM
FOUNDATIONAL | SOUL

Out of all of the **Personal Identity** areas you identified in the last chapter, which 3-5 systems feel *least* satisfying for you right now? Which areas do you want to prioritize in our work now? List them in order of priority.

1.

2.

3.

If you had to focus on *one* area to improve first, which of these systems do you feel compelled to work on first? This can be the area you identified as being least satisfying to you, but it may also be an area that you've been wanting to improve for a while, or an area you think will improve the others. Which area would you like to focus on first?

———

PERSONAL IDENTITY SYSTEM: *List your **top** priority here for easy reference.*

SELF-REFLECTION QUESTIONS

Answer the self-reflections questions below as they relate to the 3 priorities you listed above.

LIFE MANAGEMENT SYSTEM: *Copy your top priority from above.*
EMOTIONAL INTELLIGENCE SYSTEM: *Copy your top priority from above.*
PERSONAL IDENTITY SYSTEM: *Copy your top priority from above.*

Past

- What actions or beliefs seem to be a pattern in this area of your life?
- How did these beliefs or patterns become a part of your routine?
- What benefits were you getting from this behavior then? How was it serving you?

Present

- What are you getting from this now?

- How has this become a habit for you in your current life? How does it manifest now?
- How is this working for you?
- Physically
- Mentally
- Emotionally
- Spiritually
- How is this *not* working for you? Physically? Mentally? Emotionally? Spiritually?
- Do your actions and beliefs in this area align with your current values?
- Which SELF sub-personality parts are showing up for you?
- How are these parts of your SELF protecting or serving you right now?
- How are these parts holding you back right now?
- How are these actions or beliefs impacting *this* part of the system?
- How are these actions or beliefs impacting *other* parts of the system?
- What do you want to **stop** doing in this area of your life?
- What do you want to **start** doing in this area of your life?
- What do you want to **continue** doing in this area of your life?

Future

- What do you *want* this area of your life to look like?
- In a perfect world, how would it feel?

- What would need to happen to make a change in this area?
- What questions do you still have about this area of your life?
- How would a change impact your life (best guess)?
- For better?
- For worse?

NEXT STEPS

A huge part of the **Evaluate** stage is to acknowledge the grief, loss, and fear that may come up as you consider moving forward in different areas of your life. Transition is one of the hardest things we confront as humans. We're wired for certainty and consistency. Our survival instincts kick in when we face new experiences. Sometimes that means our emotions become overwhelming, which can easily make us abandon all of these positive changes we're making. Even the idea of change can be so fear-inducing that we may decide our current reality, however terrible it is, is better than the unknown.

Taking this step to acknowledge the areas of your life you'd like to change is a huge step forward. Take a little time to celebrate all of the work you've done so far. You're on the path to a Whole SELF Lifestyle!

BONUS RECAP

You can find these bonus materials in our **Bonus Library** at: www.wholeselflifestyle.com/working-parents/bonus-library.

- **Evaluation Checklist**

Also, remember you can get the **Companion Workbook** here as well: www.wholeselflifestyle.com/working-parents/companion-workbook.

15

STEP 3: (L) LIST OF SOLUTIONS

T he third step in the Whole SELF Lifestyle framework is "**L**," for **List of Solutions**.

Now that you've identified the different elements of the systems of your life and have analyzed how those areas are functioning for *you*, it's time to start identifying the *actions* you'll implement in your daily life to make improvements. You won't be making all of these changes right now. In fact, you won't be making *any* changes quite yet. Right now, we're just going to brainstorm a comprehensive list of action steps you *could* take to enhance the quality of your life. For now, just get everything out on paper, and then at the end we'll identify the best solution(s) to implement.

> *Rather than looking at information as holding the answers, I implore you to look at information as giving you the tools to find the answers yourself.* Pia Silva

SELF-REFLECTION QUESTIONS

Answer the self-reflections questions below as they relate to the **3 priorities** you listed in the last chapter.

LIFE MANAGEMENT SYSTEM: *Copy your priority here for easy reference.*
EMOTIONAL INTELLIGENCE SYSTEM: *Copy your priority here for easy reference.*
PERSONAL IDENTITY SYSTEM: *Copy your priority here for easy reference.*

- What do you **already know** about improving this area of your life?
- What **past experience** or **knowledge** can you call upon now to make changes right away, without doing any other research or learning?
- What do you just need to **implement** right now? What do you know you need to **start** doing immediately? Does anything come to mind?
- What **assumptions** are you making about changing this part of your life?
- What **resistance** are you facing in changing this part of your life? What are you **afraid** will happen if you succeed in improving this area of your life?
- What **information** are you **missing** right now? What do you need to **learn** in order to make changes in this area of your life?
- Which of the following resources do you want to follow up on to fill in gaps in knowledge or to brainstorm new ideas? Specify what you'd like to do in each area: **Google, Articles, Podcasts,**

Books, Conferences & Classes, Friends & Family, Social Media, Parenting Groups, Professional Contacts, Doctors, Therapist, Coach, Other.

———

MASTER LIST OF ACTION STEPS

Now that you've gone through your analysis and have done some research, create a list of *all* of the possible action steps you can take to improve each area of your life. This is your master list of action steps you *could* implement, based on what you know now. Make your list for *every* area before you start making any decisions, as there might be some overlap. Try to come up with at least ten ideas for each area, but keep adding as many as you need. Also feel free to come back and update these lists whenever you need to. This can be a living document to pull from.

LIFE MANAGEMENT SYSTEM: *Copy your priority here for easy reference.*
EMOTIONAL INTELLIGENCE SYSTEM: *Copy your priority here for easy reference.*
PERSONAL IDENTITY SYSTEM: *Copy your priority here for easy reference.*

———

*You can access the **List of Solutions Checklist** in the **Bonus Library** at: www.wholeselflifestyle.com/working-parents/bonus-library.*

COMMITMENTS

Now it's time to make some decisions! You should have a wide range of different solutions you can implement in order to improve the various areas of your life. Answer these questions to identify the action steps that make the most sense to implement *right now*. You'll eliminate some options, and you'll set some others aside for now - that's okay. The point here is to come up with a short list of actions you can integrate into your daily life now, without sacrificing the other areas of your life.

- Which of these action steps seem the **most doable** right now?
- Which of these action steps seem **impossible** for me right now?
- Which of these action steps seem **fun** and **enjoyable** to implement?
- Which of these action steps feel **exhausting** to even think about doing?
- Which of these action steps am I **avoiding** because I'm afraid? Is there a way to overcome this fear?
- Which of these action steps would make the biggest positive impact in *this* **area** of my life?
- Which of these action steps would make the biggest positive impact in the *other* **areas** of my life?
- Which of these action steps would **negatively impact** the other areas of my life?

- Which of these action steps would make **other options easier to implement** later if I do this now?

———

You can access the **Commitment Checklist** *in the* **Bonus Library** *at: www.wholeselflifestyle.com/working-parents/bonus-library.*

———

SETTING YOURSELF UP FOR SUCCESS

You can go through the entire Whole SELF Lifestyle process without ever seeing results if you don't make a commitment to follow through with actions. It's incredibly tempting to keep doing research to avoid really making changes in your life. But all the knowledge and insights in the world are just entertainment if you don't *do* anything with that information. Taking action is where the rubber really meets the road.

The next step of the Whole SELF Lifestyle is all about experimenting with new actions in your life: new skills, new habits, new routines, new processes, new boundaries, new conversations. Take this opportunity to choose which actions you are ready to take now. In the next chapter, you'll craft a plan to make it happen.

- What actions are you **committed** to doing in this area of your life now? Start **small** and **simple**.

SARAH ARGENAL, MA, CPC

- **How** are you going to take this action? What does it look like? Be specific.
- **When** are you going to take this action? How will this fit into your **current routine**?
- What are you going to **stop** doing in your life? How will you **eliminate** that action from your life?
- What will **prevent** you from taking this action? What will make it **difficult** to follow through?
- How can you **plan ahead** now to prevent likely obstacles or challenges?
- It's easier to replace habits than it is to remove them in your life. What unhealthy habit(s) can you **replace** right now? What **new habit** will you replace that habit with?
- How can you set yourself up for **success**? What needs to change in your **environment**, **routine** or **relationships** to ensure you stay on track?
- How can you prevent **excuses** or **procrastination** from holding you back?
- What can you do when things get **uncomfortable** or **scary**? Who can you reach out to for support in those challenging moments?

———

BONUS RECAP

You can find these bonus materials in our **Bonus Library** at: www.wholeselflifestyle.com/working-parents/bonus-library.

- **List of Solutions Checklist**
- **Commitment Checklist**

Also, remember you can get the **Companion Workbook** here as well: www.wholeselflifestyle.com/working-parents/companion-workbook.

16

STEP 4: (F) FAMILIARIZE

The fourth and final step of the Whole SELF Lifestyle framework is "**F**," for **Familiarize**. This step is often the hardest part of the Whole SELF Lifestyle for working parents, but it's also the most critical. The other three steps will give you a clear and customized roadmap to follow to improve the different systems in your life. But so far, your roadmap is still just a theory. This is the step where you *finally* get to implement all of your great plans to experience the Whole SELF Lifestyle for yourself. This step is all about gathering feedback about what *actually* works for you in your unique life, and what doesn't. This step is all about familiarizing yourself with new skills, new beliefs, new ways of being, a whole new lifestyle - one that does *not* include burnout, resentment, and frustration.

In the last step, you identified a list of action steps you are committed to taking in different areas of your life. Now it's time to go for it! Start experimenting. Try things out. Start small. Keep things simple. Do something you know will work first, so you can experience some early success and stay motivated to continue. Stay flexible. Adapt. Adjust things if they're not working. Be honest with yourself. Let go of outside pressure or opinions and look *within yourself* for answers. Listen to your intuition. See where this path takes you.

The key is to *stay observant*. There's no such thing as failure in this phase - just feedback. Take notes about what's working for you and what's not. Don't force things that simply aren't working, but don't give up too soon either. There's a sweet spot in personal growth, and this phase is all about learning what that sweet spot is for *you*. Here are some self-reflection questions to help you discover your own personal sweet spot.

 We cannot become what we want by remaining what we are. Max Depree

SELF-REFLECTION QUESTIONS

Answer the self-reflections questions below as they relate to each ACTION STEP you take.

- What did I **learn** from implementing this action step?
- Which actions felt **easy** and **light**? Which actions felt **forced** or **stressful**?
- Which action steps **contributed** to my energy levels? Which ones **depleted** my energy?
- How does this make me **feel today**? How have I felt over the last week as I've integrated this into my life?
- What do I need to do **more** of? **Less** of?

- Do I feel like my daily life is more in **alignment** with my **values**, or am I moving away from my values?
- What have I been too **afraid** to try? What's **holding me back** right now?
- Where have I fallen back into **old patterns** and **behaviors**? What triggered that backslide?
- What has been **too big** a change, too soon? Where do I need to take a step back?
- What are my most common **barriers to growth**? How do those barriers manifest in my daily life? What does it *look* and *feel* like for me?
- How has my life changed, for **better** and **worse**, since I started doing this?
- Which **skills** do I still need to develop? What's my **next step** in getting what I need?

———

*You can also access the **Keep It Or Drop It Checklist** in the **Bonus Library** at: www.wholeselflifestyle.com/ working-parents/bonus-library.*

———

*You can also access the **How to Say No Gracefully** in the **Bonus Library** at: www.wholeselflifestyle.com/working-parents/bonus-library.*

———

NEXT STEPS

This step is all about taking action so you can gain real-world self-discovery. Not every option you came up with in the last step is going to be feasible or even preferable to follow through on. Some options might be great to try now. Other options might be a great fit in the future, but not now. So pick and choose the options that are best for *you*, *your* family, *your* career, and *your* life, right now.

Don't try to make too many changes all at once. Take your time. Let new practices and perspectives sink in before switching it up again. Breathe through the discomfort and reach out for support from your circle of influence when you need it (more on this in the next chapter).

Over time, you'll familiarize yourself with new ways of being in the world. You'll familiarize yourself with new habits and new routines. You'll familiarize yourself with how *you*, as a unique individual, personally react to certain behaviors, thoughts, and feelings. You'll familiarize yourself with your limits and your preferences. You'll discover what *gives* you energy and what *depletes* your energy. You'll discover what works for *you*, in this moment, under *these circumstances*. Through this process, you'll start to see different aspects of your life shift and improve, and you'll have the self-knowledge to know how to respond to those changes. Eventually, you'll realize that you're truly living a Whole SELF Lifestyle.

BONUS RECAP

You can find these bonus materials in our **Bonus Library** at: www.wholeselflifestyle.com/working-parents/bonus-library.

- **Keep It or Drop It Checklist**
- **How to Say No Gracefully**

Also, remember you can get the **Companion Workbook** here as well: www.wholeselflifestyle.com/working-parents/ companion-workbook.

17

BUILDING YOUR CIRCLE OF INFLUENCE

Building a solid support system is one of the most important and effective things you can do when you start prioritizing balance over burnout. You don't exist in a vacuum, and it's important to have people on your side as you begin to improve your life.

This chapter will help you identify those people in your life who are the most likely to support, encourage, and inspire you to continue this journey when things get difficult. These are the people who are as interested in your best interests as their own. They can be trusted to walk with you through this transition in your life. Not all relationships are created equal, and the best way to set yourself up for success is to surround yourself with people who will support your progress.

> *As you are shifting, you will begin to realize that you are not the same person you used to be. The things you used to tolerate have become intolerable. When you once remained quiet, you are now speaking your truth. You are beginning to understand the value of your voice and there are some situations that no longer deserve your time, energy, and focus.* Mindset of Greatness

SUPPORT TO SEEK

List the names of anyone in your life who meets the description in each of the following statements. You can list just one person, or many. You can also name the same person for more than one statement. The more people you can think of the better, but don't add them just to have a lot of people on your list. They should meet this criterion completely and consistently.

- I feel comfortable being myself around them.
- I can be honest with them without being afraid of their reaction.
- I can be vulnerable and emotional with them without worrying about being judged.
- They are genuinely happy for me when I succeed or have good news.
- They offer sound advice and show good judgment in their life.
- They are honest with me when they think I'm on the wrong track.
- They encourage me to make my own decisions without influencing the outcome.

- They have achieved something in their life that I would like to achieve.
- They are kind and courteous to me and others in their life.
- There is no drama in our relationship. Disagreements are handled with respect.
- They are reliable. I can count on them to be there for me when I need them.
- They can be trusted to keep our conversations confidential. They don't gossip.
- I feel inspired to be a better person when they're around.
- I feel comfortable sharing my wins AND my failures with them.

SUPPORT TO AVOID

Not every relationship is supportive, even if it appears to be on the surface. Here are some clues that someone should *not* be a source of support as you make significant changes in your life. You don't have to exclude these people from your life altogether, but you may not want to go directly to these people as you integrate new changes in your life. Their response could have a negative impact on your overall growth. List the names of anyone in your life who meets the description in each of the following statements.

- They can be critical and judgmental.
- They tend to put my ideas down or ridicule me.
- They sometimes talk about other people behind their back.

- They have some incentive to keep me from changing (boss, spouse, parent, etc.).
- They complain without taking action to change the circumstances in their life.
- They don't understand why I would want to work so hard to change this part of my life.
- I'm not sure how they would react to my sharing "big" feelings.
- Our relationship is based more on my helping them than the other way around. There's a lack of reciprocation.
- They don't really have any experience or practical insights about this particular area I'm trying to improve.

You can also access the **Circle of Influence Checklist** *in the* **Bonus Library** *at: www.wholeselflifestyle.com/ working-parents/bonus-library.*

––––––

CIRCLE OF INFLUENCE

You should now have a short list of people you can go to for support and advice. Make a note of these people. This is your Circle of Influence. These are the best people to seek out when you need encouragement or guidance as you make changes in your life. Add their names to the **Circle of Influence Checklist** in the **Bonus Library**, as well as the different areas where they can support you most, such as career, relationships, personal growth, etc.

BONUS RECAP

You can find these bonus materials in our **Bonus Library** at: www.wholeselflifestyle.com/working-parents/bonus-library.

- **Circle of Influence Checklist**

Also, remember you can get the **Companion Workbook** here as well: www.wholeselflifestyle.com/working-parents/companion-workbook.

PART III

18

LIVING A WHOLE SELF LIFESTYLE

Now that you've gone through the entire Whole SELF Lifestyle process, the key is to continue implementing it throughout your life. Again, this is a *lifestyle*. This isn't a one-time fix. The more you explore these questions, the more deeply you'll know and understand yourself. Over time, you won't have to write the answers out, although you always can. Your instincts will take over and you'll start asking these questions in the moment, which can prevent you from getting pulled off course in your life. Use the Whole SELF Lifestyle as a tool to enhance your life... not only in the individual areas of your life, but as a *whole*.

> *Change is not a bolt of lightning that arrives with a zap. It is a bridge, built brick by brick, every day, with sweat, humanity, and slips. It is hard work, and slow work, but it can be thrilling to watch it take shape.* Sarah Hepola

WHEN TO IMPLEMENT THE WHOLE SELF LIFESTYLE

There will be a tendency to go through this process once, and then move on to the next bright and shiny self-help book. This book is designed to help you not just once, but on an *ongoing* basis. These exercises are here for you whenever you need them. Here are some specific circumstances under which the Whole SELF Lifestyle process can be particularly helpful.

————

RESTORATIVE CHECK-IN

You can go through the Whole SELF Lifestyle framework when you're struggling with burnout and need to escape survival mode. This is what I call a **Restorative Check-In**.

- When you're feeling **resentful** or **over-burdened**.
- When you're **physically sick**, **tired**, or when your health is failing.
- When you're facing or are in the midst of a **major life change**, like moving, changing jobs, or welcoming a new baby into your family (or, you know, dealing with the aftermath of a once-in-a-lifetime pandemic).
- When a part of **any of your systems shift** and change. This is a good time to determine

what adjustments might need to be made to the whole ecosystem.

- When a part of **any of your systems aren't working**. When you're feeling unfulfilled in any particular area of your life, either externally, internally, or on a fundamental level.
- When you find yourself **blaming others** for your life circumstances. Feeling like a victim or a martyr is a big sign that it's time to reclaim your power by going through this process.
- When you're feeling a sense of **failure**, **guilt**, like you're **settling**, or like you're not meeting your potential in a certain area of your life.
- When you're **comparing yourself to others**.
- When you **find yourself trying to "fix" or change other people** in order to solve your problems.
- When you're dealing with **overwhelm**, **anxiety**, **sadness**, **anger**, or any other intense emotions, and can't see a way out.

———

You can also access the ***Restorative Check-In*** in the ***Bonus Library*** at: *www.wholeselflifestyle.com/working-parents/bonus-library.*

———

PREVENTATIVE CHECK-IN

You can also set aside time on a daily or weekly or another regular basis to run through this simplified list of questions as part of your personal self-care process. This would be a **Preventative Check-In**.

- What did I **learn** today?
- What activities felt **easy** and **light**? Which activities felt **forced** or **stressful**?
- Which activities **contributed** to my energy levels? Which ones **depleted** my energy?
- Which relationships **filled me up** today? Which relationships made me **feel badly about myself** today?
- How do I **feel today**? How have I felt over the **last week**? Over the last **month**?
- What do I need to do **more** of? **Less** of?
- Do I feel like my daily life is more in **alignment** with my **values**, or am I moving away from my values?

———

*You can also access the **Preventative Check-In** in the **Bonus Library** at: www.wholeselflifestyle.com/working-parents/bonus-library.*

———

BONUS RECAP

You can find these bonus materials in our **Bonus Library**

at: www.wholeselflifestyle.com/working-parents/bonus-library.

- **Restorative Check-In**
- **Preventative Check-In**

Also, remember you can get the **Companion Workbook** here as well: www.wholeselflifestyle.com/working-parents/companion-workbook.

19

HOW TO AVOID A RELAPSE INTO BURNOUT

N ow that you're familiar with the Whole SELF Lifestyle, there are a number of ways you can go even deeper to integrate this practice into your daily life. Through your actions, you can also start to spread a new message that working parenthood doesn't need to be a miserable and exhausting experience. It's time for us to create a new lifestyle for working parents that is understanding, fulfilling, and allows each person to live the life that's most effective for them. Broad cultural adoption of this new lifestyle starts with *you*.

> *Life isn't about waiting for the storm to pass. It's about learning to dance in the rain.* Vivian Greene

HOW TO MAINTAIN THESE CHANGES

Here are a number of recommendations to help you integrate the changes you've made into your life in deeper and new ways. Pick and choose any of these options, depending on your needs. Come back to this list often and keep trying new things. Discover what works best for *you*.

1. **Refer to this book** whenever you need a little life upgrade... in a *single* area of your life, or in *all* areas of your life. Use this framework whenever you need guidance or are feeling burned out.

2. **Integrate these activities into your daily routine.** Use the **Bonus Library** materials to enhance your life experiences and relationships.

3. **Download the Companion Workbook** from Amazon for ongoing support. Refer to those exercises whenever you need to get back on track.

4. **Go through the Whole SELF Lifestyle framework with your spouse, partner, or family**. Share your answers and brainstorm ways to integrate what you learn into your marriage, your parenting, and your family experience.

5. **Integrate this into the work you're doing with your therapist, coach, or mentor.** Use your responses to these exercises as areas to address your particular challenges and needs in more depth.

6. **Start a Book Club or Whole SELF Lifestyle™ Circle** with your friends or colleagues. Go through the exercises together and discuss your responses with a supportive group. Try this once, or schedule regular check-ins to stay on track.

7. **Listen to the Working Parent Resource Podcast** to explore all of the topics we discuss here in more depth, and to receive updated information on the Whole SELF Lifestyle. You can listen at www.argenalinstitute.com/podcast, or on all of the major listening apps such as Apple Podcasts, Stitcher, Spotify, Google Play, and iHeartRadio.

8. **Connect with me on social media** to keep the conversation going. My favorite place to connect is on LinkedIn.

9. **Interview me for your podcast, show or article.** Spread the word about the Whole SELF Lifestyle to your friends, clients, co-workers, and community. Visit www. wholeselflifestyle.com/working-parents/ consultation to schedule a **free consultation** with me to discuss further.

10. **Apply to work with me privately, either individually or in one of my group programs or events**. Dive deeper and receive personalized support. Visit www. wholeselflifestyle.com/working-parents/ consultation to schedule a **free consultation** with me to discuss further.

11. **Integrate the Whole SELF Lifestyle framework in the following group settings**. Visit www.wholeselflifestyle.com/ working-parents/consultation to schedule a **free consultation** with me to discuss further.

- Company Training

- Parenting Groups
- Association Meetings
- Industry Events
- Conferences
- Wellness Retreats
- High schools and Universities
- Business and Graduate Schools
- Non-Profit Institutions

20

A NEW FUTURE

"Cheers, honey!" Joey and I clinked our glasses of champagne. We were on another lunch date just before the lockdown, this time to celebrate our seventh wedding anniversary. A lot has changed since those early days of parenthood. Today, we're in a very different place mentally, emotionally, and geographically.

After a couple of years trying to improve our lifestyle, Joey and I came to the difficult realization that we were never going to be able to have the kind of life we wanted in the San Francisco Bay Area. Even after making small changes to our daily routine, it just wasn't enough to build the kind of life we truly wanted. A lot of things improved, but not enough for us.

Joey and I both coordinated with our companies to transfer our work and our family to San Diego. I kept my job and moved to my firm's office in downtown San Diego. Joey continued his position with the same company and worked remotely from home. Right after we moved, I also launched what is now The Argenal Institute, where we continue to support the mental and emotional well-being of working parents.

Wanting to expand our family was a large part of our decision to ultimately leave the Bay Area. The cost of putting two children in full-time childcare, moving to a larger house, and dealing with an even longer commute were the proverbial straws that broke the camel's back. We realized the stress of having two kids in the San Francisco area may be manageable, but it wasn't what we wanted for our family. We knew the financial and energetic strain we felt with one child would be compounded if we expanded our family. That was the opposite of what we wanted. San Diego seemed to be a good compromise. It was close enough to San Francisco that we could visit whenever we wanted, and it alleviated just about everything we struggled with in our daily lives.

After we became settled into our new home in San Diego, we started trying to conceive a second baby. A year and three rounds of fertility treatments later, we finally got pregnant. Our second little boy, Weston, joined our family in 2017. A couple of years after that, Joey was offered a position at a company he loved, which meant moving from San Diego to Austin, Texas. We were sad to leave San Diego, but we also looked forward to being closer to my family, experience even more financial security, have more time with the kids, and continue to shape our lives around our core family values.

Shortly after we moved to Austin, we also made the decision to homeschool our kids. We've had to adapt what that looks like since the pandemic started, but Beckett is still flourishing in school, and Weston follows his big brother around like a shadow. They're sweet and kind to each other (unless Weston wants the toy Beckett is playing with – then it is *on*). They look out for each other in a way that melts my heart.

We prioritize self-directed learning in our curriculum, so there's a lot of freedom and experimentation. We blend a rich variety of community programs, project-based education, extracurricular activities, online courses, technology and apps, political and social justice causes, and character development into their learning. We also integrate travel and exploration of new areas into their education however we can.

The Argenal Institute has turned into my primary work focus, although I also still do some litigation consulting and project management on a freelance basis. I now live a "portfolio life," a phrase I first heard from the writer Jeff Goins to describe someone who integrates a variety of sources of income and professional outlets into their career.

Today I spread the message of the Whole SELF Lifestyle through writing books, articles for outlets such as *Working Mother*, *Healthline* and *Thrive Global*, or on my blog, producing my podcast, appearing on various media outlets, facilitating workshops and webinars, and private consulting. I also coach other authors who serve working parents and want to publish their own books. I work more than a full-time schedule, but I work from home 100% of the time and have complete control over my schedule which makes all the difference. I have the flexibility to work when and how I want. My focus has shifted almost exclusively to the people and activities that are most important to me.

Here's what a typical day in our pre-coronavirus life looked like. Not much has changed during the pandemic, except Joey works in our home office exclusively these days and the boys' social activities are all virtual now. We've made a lot of adjustments since those early days of working parenthood.

- Joey starts work early, but Beckett, Weston, and I wake up whenever we're no longer tired, usually around 7:00 or 7:30 a.m. We all snuggle on the couch and chat while I enjoy my morning coffee.
- The boys eat breakfast, get dressed, and play a game or watch an educational show while I catch up on the news and get organized for the day.
- Around 8:00 a.m., Beckett and Weston do some free play while I tidy up the house or do some work. Most mornings, I'll do a workout while the kids play. When it's nice outside, we'll all go for a walk or bike ride on the nature trail by our house.
- Later in the morning, we'll head out on an adventure together or meet up with friends. Other days Beckett has an activity or a class. Some days I have client calls and interviews, so the boys head off to a local kids' group to play with friends and do art projects. Other days, Weston, Beckett and I will work on an educational project together. We'll read about the history of the world, do a science experiment, practice handwriting and reading, or do some math activities. Every morning is a little different.
- Around noon, we'll clean up the house again (it's an ongoing effort) and make lunch together. Beckett does his chores and helps me with lunch.
- After lunch, we have quiet time. We turn down the lights. Beckett watches a documentary, does some coding on the computer, plays games on his iPad, builds with LEGO, or gets into a project while Weston watches a movie, colors, does a puzzle, crafts with playdough or plays quietly. I

focus on work for a couple more hours. Around
3:00 p.m., the boys head outside to play.

- After outside time, Beckett will choose another
  school project to work on. Weston either gets
  involved in the project too, depending on what it
  is, or he plays on his own. I continue working
  while supervising the boys. Sometimes I move
  around the house with my laptop, and other times
  I work in my office, which is next to the playroom
  so the kids can play or work nearby. Other times I
  work on my treadmill desk, which is in our
  homeschool room so the kids can play or work in
  there. When the weather is nice, the boys play in
  the backyard while I work on the patio. We move
  around a lot, depending on what we're all doing.
  We've set up our home and our schedule to
  maximize our freedom and options.
- Joey usually gets home from work between 4:00
  and 6:00 p.m. depending on his workday. If he's
  in the middle of a big project, he'll continue
  working in our home office. If he's finished up his
  work for the day, he'll play with the boys or build
  LEGO with Beckett. Other days we all go for a
  walk around the neighborhood or play at our
  community pool if it's hot.
- Around 5:00 p.m., Joey or I will start preparing
  dinner, depending on who still has work to wrap
  up. Sometimes Beckett will finish up whatever
  school activities he's been working on at the
  kitchen table, and Weston will paint or color.
  Other times the boys will play together or with
  one of us.
- We all hang out together as a family, play a

game, relax in the backyard, or watch a show after dinner. I'll either finish up my work or play with the boys while Joey cleans the kitchen (or vice versa). It's pretty fluid based on what's going on for each of us that day and what we feel like doing. We have a lot of options to choose from.

- At 7:00 p.m., both of the boys shower or take a bath. Weston goes to bed while Beckett plays a game, does a puzzle, watches a movie, or just relaxes. Beckett heads to bed around 8:30 p.m.
- After the boys are in bed, Joey and I usually watch a show together or just talk. In the warmer seasons, we'll sit out on our back porch with a glass of wine, listen to music, and chat.
- Joey and I usually head to bed around 10:00 or 11:00 p.m. Now that the boys are getting older, we all (mostly) sleep through the night too, which makes a huge difference.

This schedule is a much better fit for where we are in our lives today. I'm sure it won't always look like this and I know it's not what everyone would choose, but it works for us right now. We've made a series of conscious decisions to craft this reality. It hasn't always been easy, but it's definitely been worth it. Joey and I have integrated the Whole SELF Lifestyle into our individual lives, and it continues to drive our decisions as a family.

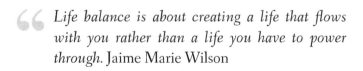

Life balance is about creating a life that flows with you rather than a life you have to power through. Jaime Marie Wilson

THE WHOLE SELF LIFESTYLE CHANGED MY LIFE

Here's what has changed in my life as a direct result of living a Whole SELF Lifestyle:

- My physical and mental wellness have both improved.
- My marriage with Joey has deepened and strengthened, even through some of the most challenging times in our marriage.
- Joey and I are giving our children healthier role models for life. We don't stress out nearly as much, and we prioritize what's most meaningful to us.
- We have stronger and more connected relationships with each other, our kids, our close friends, and our extended family.
- We have a lot more fun and enjoy our lives more than we used to. We embrace these precious moments with our kids.
- I derive my motivation and self-worth from within, rather than what everyone else wants from me. The things I do, think, and pursue originate from *within* me, not *outside* of me.
- My sense of self-awareness has led to an acceptance of reality as it *actually* is, and not how I *want* it to be. This has resulted in lower levels of stress and resentment. I now focus on what's within my control and let everything else go for the moment.
- I've stopped blaming others for what's not working in my life. By reclaiming responsibility

for my future, I've also regained the power to make choices that will lead to more fulfillment, peace, and joy.

- I've forgiven myself for making mistakes. I'm no longer afraid to be "found out," which liberates me to bring my full self to all situations in my life without hiding behind a mask or a façade. I no longer go through that complicated and exhausting calculation of how to please others. I've stopped manipulating situations to control how others perceive me. I am simply *me* in every moment, regardless of the circumstances.

- I now respond to life's joys and challenges rather than merely "powering through" to survive my day. I rely on a variety of tools to manage my emotions, big and small, which allows me to tap back into my whole experience of life. I can *feel* all parts of my experience. I'm no longer numb to the good parts because I'm scared of the hard parts. I see life as an adventure with a lot of ups and downs, and plenty of life lessons mixed in.

WE CAN CHANGE THE WORLD THROUGH THE WHOLE SELF LIFESTYLE

These benefits of the Whole SELF Lifestyle aren't unique to me. Over the years, I've seen this process work the same kind of magic in many different lives.

The pervasive feelings of stress, hopelessness, and burnout in our society won't change until we become healthier as individuals. It starts within each of us. As we integrate the principles of the Whole SELF Lifestyle into our own lives, we'll become equipped to improve our reality, as well as that of the people around us.

That said, becoming self-aware isn't all about prioritizing *self* over the collective at all costs. Being a positive member of society involves keeping the fate of the community in mind. When we have a robust sense of self, we naturally embrace the compassion, empathy, and motivation necessary for a healthy and supportive society. The Whole SELF Lifestyle starts within, but it doesn't end there. As you integrate the Whole SELF Lifestyle into your daily life, here are a few other ways you can improve not only your own life, but the world around you too:

- As you explore the depths of your identity, you'll be more prepared to leverage that unique mix of qualities only *you* have to improve your world - at home, at work, and everywhere in between.
- You can eliminate that fractured feeling that comes from trying to be too many things to too many people in too many different situations. You'll redistribute all of that energy back to yourself. You'll start to operate more deliberately from a deeper sense of self and purpose. That allows you to offer the best of yourself to the people around you. As you become healthier, you'll naturally become a better partner, parent, friend, and member of your community.
- You'll replace that impulse to find a quick fix with a more comprehensive perspective of your life. You'll begin to see personal development as an ongoing, messy, but ultimately far more fulfilling

SARAH ARGENAL, MA, CPC

practice that leads to a healthier and happier lifestyle.

- You'll return to having real connection and intimacy in your relationships - at home, at work, and in society in general. You'll participate in less conflict and more understanding within your family, in the workplace, and in your community.

- You'll leverage the vast array of information that exists out there in an *intentional* way, rather than feeling bombarded by information, opinions, and advice. You can reject the "guru culture" that can be so tempting and start trusting your internal wisdom. Your instincts and your values will be your guide as you pick and choose the advice that's best for you and your family.

- You can opt out of measuring your self-worth by other people's definitions and expectations. You can refer to your deepest values as your true North Star.

- You don't have to numb out in your life anymore. You don't have to try to avoid the painful parts of life. Instead, you can use your valuable time to recharge, fill your cup, and experience more meaningful moments.

- You can let go of the fear, anxiety, and paralysis that comes with uncertainty. You can start to embrace life as it comes because you'll trust you have the tools and skills to handle whatever comes at you. You'll see challenges as opportunities for personal growth. You'll see a conflict with others as a way to not only strengthen your relationship but as a way to become an even better version of yourself.

- Together we can increase tolerance and inclusion for all walks of life in our communities as we embrace each other's differences, unique qualities and gifts. As we come to know, love, and accept our full selves, it's much easier to do the same for others.
- You can look back on your life with no regrets. The Whole SELF Lifestyle allows you to soak in those precious moments with your kids when they're little, build a stable and loving partnership with your spouse, and take care of yourself in each moment.

Self-awareness isn't a requirement to *survive* your life, but it *is* a requirement to *enjoy* your life. The more you know yourself, the more you'll enjoy this adventure called working parenthood. I hope the Whole SELF Lifestyle offers the inspiration and structure to help you kick off your own journey of self-discovery.

21
A SNAPSHOT IN TIME

There's an exercise I've been doing since I was a teenager. I didn't explicitly set out to do this initially, but it has become a consistent practice in my life over time.

The first time I remember doing this exercise was the day before I moved away to college. My bags were packed, and I was ready to move on to the next chapter of my life. I was leaving the familiar landscape of my childhood forever. I would miss my family and friends, of course, but I had been planning my "escape" since I was a kid. I couldn't wait to finally move on to bigger and better things.

I grew up in the remote northern California mountain town of Mt. Shasta, which sits about an hour south of the Oregon border. At 14,179 feet, this awe-inspiring mountain is surrounded by thick forests, natural freshwater lakes, and ice-cold rivers.

On my last day as a Mt. Shasta resident, I felt nostalgic. I was ready to move on, but I was also quite aware that the rest of my life was utterly unknown. I felt the excitement and possibility mixed with the trepidation that comes with a significant life change. To honor this big life shift, I was inspired to visit some of the most memorable scenes of my childhood before I took off on my first honest-to-goodness adult adventure.

With my music blasting and the car windows down, I headed up and down the windy mountain roads. I took the scenic route to my favorite spot in the area, Castle Lake. I recalled swimming across the lake with my sisters countless times, a perfect 45-minute swim each way. Then I passed my other favorite spot, Siskiyou Lake, where I spent hours playing on a rope swing with my friends and sunbathing on the beach in the summer. I passed tennis courts, old hang-outs, and the college theater where I met some of my closest friends. I headed toward Emerald Falls, a natural waterfall that led to a deep green swimming hole.

While I drove, I reflected on my years growing up in this small town. I thought about all of the arguments I had with my siblings and parents, but also the philosophical conversations we had around the dinner table. I recalled all of the laughs I had with my friends and classmates. I was reminded of old boyfriends who had moved on in their own lives. Like a movie reel, I reflected on the most poignant moments of my life up to that point. I felt grateful for the life I already had and excited for the journey I was about to embark upon.

At some point on that tour, it occurred to me that there would be a day in the not too distant future when I would look back and remember *that moment*.... that *exact* moment. I knew as I drove from lake to lake, up and down the mountain and through the woods, that I was taking a *snapshot in time* that I would revisit someday. Just as I remembered the most pivotal moments of my childhood, I knew eventually I would look back and recall *that* moment. Today, I remember that drive as if it were yesterday.

———

> To find peace, you have to be willing to lose your connection with the people, places and things that create all the noise. Honi Bee

Over the years I've learned to integrate this "snapshot in time" exercise into my daily life. Now and then, I stop all of the *doing*. I'll be as still and as quiet as I can, and I'll consciously remember *that moment* for the sole purpose of coming back to it someday in the future when I'm an even more complete version of myself. I imagine I'll look back on that particular moment with hindsight I don't have yet. I get curious about what I'll think of that memory as Future Me.

I remember the moment nearly twenty years ago when I swung in a hammock on a beach in Thailand. I'd snuck away from the loud music and cacophony of voices from the restaurant behind me. The noises faded. The sun was setting. The light, warm breeze was comfortable. After a month of life-changing solo adventures, I was heading home to the United States a few days later. I knew this would be one of my last moments of quiet on a tropical beach before heading home to the city. I bottled up the feeling of pure peace and solitude to take back home. I still revisit that moment when I need to calm myself or when I meditate.

A week after that, my first day back to work after my sabbatical in Thailand, my colleagues stopped me just outside our building in the financial district in San Francisco. They told me to turn around and go home. The twin towers in New York had just collapsed and the whole area was being evacuated. They didn't know if other attacks were planned, and we needed to leave the downtown area immediately.

The rest of that week was a blur of uncertainty, fear, and mass memorials. But I clearly remember the moment when two commercial airliners hit the twin towers on the news, and then later the Pentagon, then another crashed into a Pennsylvania field. I, like so many others, grasped the fragility of life as I watched those towers crumble. Those moments are burned into my mind forever. How I felt at that moment, that snapshot in time, came roaring back to me as I visited the 9/11 memorial in New York City for the first time many years later.

Around my thirtieth birthday, I walked along another quiet beach in Capitola, California. I had just gone through another unexpected breakup with yet another boyfriend. I had no idea why I kept choosing partners who weren't healthy for me. I was wallowing in self-pity, and I had the distinct feeling that time was running out for me to have a family of my own. Then I had a vision. I saw myself years in the future, returning to that exact beach with my loving husband and our two kids. Many years later, I did go back to that beach with my loving husband and our two boys. Those are both precious snapshots in time for me. My own personal "before and after" pictures that generate a certainty of faith when times are hard and I convince myself that difficulty means I'm on the wrong path in life.

————

As I sit here working on this book, our family is complying with quarantine guidelines to slow the spread of a deadly global disease. We've been isolated in our homes for months already, and we currently have no idea when it will end.

Many families I know are anxious about the disruption to their busy lives, and rightfully so. They dread being home indefinitely with their families. The chaos of everyone's lives is being canceled in every way, and modern working families are struggling to cope with the lack of distraction, as well as the profound uncertainty about the future.

As I watch people on social media and news reports respond to these unprecedented circumstances in different ways, my attention is brought back to my kids. Beckett has grabbed a stack of blankets and every last pillow in the house to build a cozy bed on our living room floor. When it's done, he and Weston get comfortable and chat about the differences between their respective Hot Wheels cars. They goof around and snuggle together. They laugh and tease each other.

The juxtaposition was stark. Outside, society as we know it has been paused. Inside our home, my kids are going about their day as though nothing has changed. They reminded me that it's important to laugh and enjoy the people we love most, even when the world seems bleak. The simplicity of their interaction gave me a feeling of hope and joy that I desperately needed in such a confusing and overwhelming time. It's a sweet moment I want to remember for the rest of my life. I add that snapshot in time to all of the others of my life. Someday, long before I'm ready, these little boys will be all grown up and off living their own lives (God, willing). If I'm lucky, I'll have an abundance of meaningful snapshots in time to return to.

ENJOY THESE PRECIOUS YEARS OF YOUR LIFE

At the end of our lives, all we have is our relationships and our memories. It's easy to take these early years of working parenthood for granted. The chaos of life with kids can feel so demanding and tedious. Changing diapers. Responding to our two hundredth work email of the day. Cooking another dinner, which will probably go uneaten by picky kids. Folding the 3,439th load of laundry. The days can feel like a nonstop grind.

There will be a day in your not too distant future when you'll look back at *this moment* of your life and you'll remember... *something*. My hope is that you'll look back with fond memories of the giggles, the conversations, and the cuddles. I want you to look back with the certainty that you made the *most* of these moments, because the only thing we know for certain right now is soon those moments *will* be gone. I hope you'll pause in those moments of chaos and prioritize love and connection. I invite you to *choose* the life you *want*, over the life you feel you're required to tolerate. Will there be bad days? Of course, that's part of life. But only *you* are in a position to ensure the heartwarming experiences outnumber the tiresome ones. Reclaim that power for yourself today. Remind yourself of your power often.

I challenge you to release old notions of work-life balance, and instead embrace the Whole SELF Lifestyle as an intentional practice in your life as a working parent. I invite you to *enjoy* these precious years with your family. Take this opportunity to foster the memories and the relationships that will live in your heart today, at the end of your life, and every day in between.

APPENDIX

RECOMMENDED RESOURCES
APPENDIX 1

Some of the resources listed below are referenced throughout this book. Others weren't referenced specifically in this book, but I've found them to be incredibly helpful as a working parent so I've included them as well. These Recommended Resources have been added to the Bonus Library. That version may be updated over time with additional resources, so there may be some minor differences in the list you see in the Bonus Library.

BOOKS

- Alcorn, K. 2013. Maxed Out: American Moms on the Brink. New York, NY: Seal Press.
- Brown, B. 2010. The Gifts of Imperfection: Let Go of Who You Think You're Supposed to Be and Embrace Who You Are. Center City, MN: Hazelden Publishing.
- Burke Harris, Dr. N. 2020. The Deepest Well: Healing the Long-Term Effects of Childhood.

- Denworth, L. (2020, January 28). Friendship: The Evolution, Biology, and Extraordinary Power of Life's Fundamental Bond. New York, NY: W. W. Norton & Company.
- Adversity. London, United Kingdom: Bluebird Books.
- Eyal, N. (2019, September 10). Indistractable: How to Control Your Attention and Choose Your Life. Dallas, TX: BenBella Books.
- Gladwell, M. 2008. Outliers: The Story of Success. New York, NY: Hachette Book Group.
- Gottman, J., Schwartz Gottman, J. 2007. And Baby Makes Three: The Six-Step Plan for Preserving Marital Intimacy and Rekindling Romance After Baby Arrives. New York, NY: Harmony Books.
- Huffington, A. 2014. Thrive: The Third Metric to Redefining Success and Creating a Life of Well-Being, Wisdom, and Wonder. New York, NY: Harmony Books.
- Manne, K. 2017. Down Girl: The Logic of Misogyny. Cary, NC: Oxford University Press.
- Markham, L. 2012. Peaceful Parent, Happy Kids: How to Stop Yelling and Start Connecting. London, United Kingdom: Penguin Group.
- McKeown, G. 2014. Essentialism: The Disciplined Pursuit of Less. New York, NY: Random House LLC.
- McNamee, R. 2019. Zucked: Waking Up to the Facebook Catastrophe. London, United Kingdom: Penguin Group.
- Newport, C. (2019, February 5). Digital Minimalism: Choosing a Focused Life in a Noisy

World. London, United Kingdom: Penguin Group (USA) LLC.

- Nichols, T. (2018, October 1). The Death of Expertise: The Campaign against Established Knowledge and Why it Matters. Oxford, England, UK: Oxford University Press.
- Rodsky, E. (2019, October 1). Fair Play: A Game-Changing Solution for When You Have Too Much to Do (and More Life to Live). New York, NY: G.P. Putnam's Sons.
- Sandberg, S. 2013. Lean In: Women, Work, and the Will to Lead. New York, NY: Random House LLC.
- Siegel , D., Payne Bryson, T. 2011. The Whole Brain Child: 12 Revolutionary Strategies to Nurture Your Child's Developing Mind. New York, NY: Delacorte Press.
- Stoddard, J. 2020. Be Mighty: A Woman's Guide to Liberation from Anxiety, Worry, and Stress Using Mindfulness and Acceptance. Oakland, CA: New Harbinger Publications.
- Stromberg, L. 2019. Work, Pause, Thrive: How to Pause for Parenthood Without Ruining Your Career. Dallas, TX: BenBella Books.
- Tsabary, S. 2010. The Conscious Parent: Transforming Ourselves, Empowering Our Children. Vancouver, Canada: Namaste Publishing.
- Zuckerman, E. 2013. Digital Cosmopolitans: Why We Think the Internet Connects Us, Why It Doesn't, and How to Rewire It. New York, NY: W. W. Norton & Company.

ARTICLES & REPORTS

- Arends, B. (2019, April 22). Why the Middle Class is Shrinking. *Market Watch*. Retrieved from https://www.marketwatch.com/story/why-the-middle-class-is-shrinking-2019-04-12
- Argenal, S. (2019, December 9). 3 Skills that Help Me Navigate Working Parenthood. *Healthline*. Retrieved from https://www.healthline.com/health/parenting/3-surprising-skills-that-help-me-navigate-working-parenthood
- Argenal, S. (2019, June 26). Why Focusing on Self-Care Isn't Fixing Burnout for Working Parents. *Working Mother*. Retrieved from https://www.workingmother.com/why-focusing-on-self-care-isnt-fixing-burnout-for-working-moms
- Baer, D. (2014, July 3). New Study Destroys Malcolm Gladwell's 10,000 Hour Rule. *Business Insider*. Retrieved from https://www.businessinsider.com/new-study-destroys-malcolm-gladwells-10000-rule-2014-7
- Burn-out an 'Occupational Phenomenon': International Classification of Diseases. (2019, May 28). *World Health Organization*. Retrieved from https://www.who.int/mental_health/evidence/burn-out/en/
- Carrell, R. (2019, August 15). Let's Share Women's Mental Load. *Forbes*. Retrieved from https://www.forbes.com/sites/rachelcarrell/2019/08/15/lets-share-womens-mental-load/#52b95a566bd6
- Casselman, B. (2019, May 2). Why Wages Are Finally Rising, 10 Years After the Recession. *The*

New York Times. Retrieved from https://www.nytimes.com/2019/05/02/business/economy/wage-growth-economy.html

- Desilver, D. (2018, August 7). For Most U.S. Workers, Real Wages Have Barely Budged in Decades. *Pew Research Center*. Retrieved from https://www.pewresearch.org/fact-tank/2018/08/07/for-most-us-workers-real-wages-have-barely-budged-for-decades/

- Downey, M. (2020 April 1). This is Not Home Schooling, Distance Learning or Online Schooling. *Atlanta Journal Constitution*. Retrieved from https://www.ajc.com/blog/get-schooled/opinion-this-not-home-schooling-distance-learning-online-schooling/b9rNnK77eyVLhsRMhaqZwL/amp.html

- Facts & Statistics. (n.d.). *Anxiety and Depression Association of America*. Retrieved from https://adaa.org/about-adaa/press-room/facts-statistics

- Facts About Bullying (n.d.). *Stop Bullying*. Retrieved from https://www.stopbullying.gov/media/facts/index.html

- Fox, M. (2018, May 10). Major Depression on the Rise Among Everyone, New Data Shows. *NBC News*. Retrieved from https://www.nbcnews.com/health/health-news/major-depression-rise-among-everyone-new-data-shows-n873146

- Francis, L. (2019, December 13). Dads Are Experiencing the Motherhood Penalty. That's Not Good. *Fatherly*. Retrieved from https://www.fatherly.com/love-money/relationships/motherhood-penalty-dads/

- Friedman, Z. (2019, January 11). 78% of Workers Live Paycheck to Paycheck. *Forbes*. Retrieved from https://www.forbes.com/sites/zackfriedman/2019/01/11/live-paycheck-to-paycheck-government-shutdown/#5040a5ac4f10

- Fuller, J., Manjari, R. (2019, January 17). The Caring Company. *Harvard Business Review*. Retrieved from https://www.hbs.edu/managing-the-future-of-work/Documents/The_Caring_Company.pdf

- Garcia-Alonso, J., Krentz, M., Lovich, D., Quickenden, S., Brooks Taplett, F. (2019, April 10). Lightening the Mental Load that Holds Women Back. *Boston Consulting Group*. Retrieved from https://www.bcg.com/publications/2019/lightening-mental-load-holds-women-back.aspx

- Gassam, J. (2019 March 23). Why Leaning In Doesn't Apply to Women of Color. *Forbes*. Retrieved from https://www.forbes.com/sites/janicegassam/2019/03/23/why-leaning-in-has-not-worked-for-women-of-color/

- Henley, D. (2020 February 16). How to Thrive In Complexity and Chaos. *Forbes*. Retrieved from https://www.forbes.com/sites/dedehenley/2020/02/16/embrace-the-chaos-what-you-can-learn-in-complex-environments/#22b504b44db9

- Huffington, A. (2019 March 25). The United States of Stress. *Thrive Global*. Retrieved from https://thriveglobal.com/stories/stress-crisis-sanjay-gupta-hbo-united-states/amp/

- Illing, S. (2020, March 7). What We Get Wrong

About Misogyny. *Vox*. Retrieved from https://
www.vox.com/identities/2017/12/5/
16705284/metoo-weinstein-misogyny-trump-
sexism

- Jones, M. (2017, October 19). 11 Billion Reasons
  the Self-Help Industry Doesn't Want You to
  Know The Truth About Happiness. *Inc*.
  Retrieved from https://www.inc.com/matthew-
  jones/11-billion-reasons-self-help-industry-
  doesnt-want-you-to-know-truth-about-
  happiness.html
- Kindelan, K. (2020 March 26). Women More
  Stressed, Burdened by Coronavirus Than Men,
  Poll Finds. 5 Ways to Change That. *Good
  Morning America*. Retrieved from https://www.
  goodmorningamerica.com/wellness/story/
  women-stressed-burdened-coronavirus-men-poll-
  finds-ways-69787591
- Levitin, D. (2015 January 18). Why the Modern
  World is Bad For Your Brain. The Guardian.
  Retrieved from https://www.theguardian.com/
  science/2015/jan/18/modern-world-bad-for-
  brain-daniel-j-levitin-organized-mind-
  information-overload
- Maldonado, Camilo. (2018, July 24). The Cost of
  College Increasing Nearly 8 Times Faster than
  Wages. *Forbes*. Retrieved from https://www.
  forbes.com/sites/camilomaldonado/2018/07/
  24/price-of-college-increasing-almost-8-times-
  faster-than-wages/#3bb7f23e66c1
- Morgan, W. V. (2017, September 1). How Social
  Media is Killing your Oxytocin Levels and
  Keeping you from Being your Happiest Self.

Medium. Retrieved from https://medium.com/@whitneyvmorgan/how-social-media-is-killing-your-oxytocin-levels-and-keeping-you-from-being-your-happiest-self-89e327a375c3

- New Research Shows the 'Mental Load' is Real and Significantly Impacts Working Mothers Both at Home and Work. (2010, October 13). *Business Wire*. Retrieved from https://www.businesswire.com/news/home/20171220005984/en/New-Research-Shows-%E2%80%9CMental-Load%E2%80%9D-Real-Significantly
- Peck, S. (2019 Jan 24). Workplaces Aren't Paying Attention to the Growing Caretaking Crisis, And It's Costing Them Talent. *Forbes*. Retrieved from https://www.forbes.com/sites/sarahkathleenpeck/2019/01/24/workplaces-arent-paying-attention-to-the-growing-caretaking-crisis-and-its-costing-them-talent/?fbclid=IwAR3zDj9X6nozuMAhcahZANUyYD3IGGe0lı1N_71mLM6JoioYc4X5NcabhMo#6e54a5091677
- Reigeluth, C., Bathany, B., Olson, J. (2019, December 2). Comprehensive Systems Design: A New Educational Technology. *NATO Advanced Science Institute Series*. Retrieved from https://link.springer.com/content/pdf/bfm%3A978-3-642-58035-2%2F1.pdf
- Rittenberry, E. (2019, February 1). The American Life is Killing You. *Medium*. Retrieved from https://medium.com/@erikrittenberry/the-american-life-is-killing-you-9e7e68135f4a
- Selingo, J. (2018, June 2). How the Great Recession Changed the Job Market Forever for

College Grads. *The Washington Post*. Retrieved from https://www.washingtonpost.com/news/grade-point/wp/2018/06/01/how-the-great-recession-changed-the-job-market-forever-for-college-grads/

- Simmons, M. (2019, January 18). Most People Think This is a Good Habit, But It's Actually Causing Brain Damage. *Mental Model Club*. Retrieved from https://mentalmodelclub.com/mentalmodelclub/junk-learning-billionaire-mind-4.html

- Simon, L. (2018 March 14). How Information Overload Affects the Brain. *PsychCentral*. Retrieved from https://pro.psychcentral.com/how-information-overload-affects-the-brain/

- Simon, M. (2020 March 19). Women and the Hidden Burden of the Coronavirus. *The Hill*. Retrieved from https://thehill.com/changing-america/respect/equality/488509-the-hidden-burden-of-the-coronavirus-on-women

- Skenazy, L., Gray, P. (2020 March 29). Coronavirus is Providing the Course Correction Kids Desperately Needed. *New York Post*. Retrieved from https://nypost.com/2020/03/29/coronavirus-is-providing-the-course-correction-kids-desperately-needed/

- Vox Creative. (2020, February 13). Why You Should Value Privacy, Even If You Have Nothing to Hide. *Vox*. Retrieved from https://www.vox.com/ad/21136449/privacy-data-technology?fbclid=IwAR2WzBQzGKhHGN85vMYkVoWEIKWPGp8sI_DfSxECYa6VbamGYTY9-YZUtuY

- Winerman, Lea. (2019, January). By the Numbers: An Alarming Rise in Suicide. *American Psychological Association*. Retrieved from https://www.apa.org/monitor/2019/01/numbers
- Zalis, S. (2019 February 22). The Motherhood Penalty: Why We're Losing Our Best Talent to Caregiving. *Forbes*. Retrieved from https://www.forbes.com/sites/shelleyzalis/2019/02/22/the-motherhood-penalty-why-were-losing-our-best-talent-to-caregiving/

PODCASTS

- Ables, M., Wilson, A. (Producers). What Fresh Hell [Audio podcast]. Retrieved from https://www.whatfreshhellpodcast.com/
- Argenal, S. (Producer). Working Parent Resource Podcast [Audio podcast]. Retrieved from https://argenalinstitute.com/podcast
- Babauta, L. (Producer). Zen Habits Radio [Audio producer]. Retrieved from http://www.zenhabitsradio.com/
- Brown, B. (Producer). Unlocking Us [Audio podcast]. Retrieved from https://brenebrown.com/podcast/introducing-unlocking-us/
- Chauvin, H. (Producer). The Mom Is In Control Podcast [Audio podcast]. Retrieved from http://heatherchauvin.com/podcast
- Ching, R. (Producer). The Unburdened Life [Audio podcast]. Retrieved from https://www.rebeccaching.com/podcast
- Ellsworth, B. (Producer). Work from Your Happy

Place [Audio podcast]. Retrieved from https://www.workfromyourhappyplace.com/podcast/

- Francis, M., Powers, S. (Producers). The Mom Hour [Audio Podcast]. Retrieved from https://themomhour.com/episodes/
- Hennessy, K. (Producer). Mother Like a Boss [Audio podcast]. Retrieved from http://www.kendrahennessy.com/podcast
- Hill, D., Schonbrun, Y., Sorenson, D., Stoddard, J. (Producers). Psychologists Off The Clock [Audio podcast]. Retrieved from https://www.offtheclockpsych.com/episodes
- Koh, C., Dornfest, A. (Producers). The Edit Your Life Show [Audio podcast]. Retrieved from http://www.edityourlifeshow.com/episodes/
- Lansbury, J. (Producer). Unruffled [Audio podcast]. Retrieved from https://www.janetlansbury.com/podcast-audio/
- Lumanlan, J. (Producer). Your Parenting Mojo Podcast [Audio podcast]. Retrieved from https://yourparentingmojo.com/episodes/
- Marinovich, A. (Producer). Learn with Less [Audio podcast]. Retrieved from https://learnwithless.com/category/podcast/
- Marks, Dr. Tracey (Producer). Beyond Burnout [Audio podcast]. Retrieved from http://beyondburnout.com/category/podcast/
- Shepard, D. (Producer). Armchair Expert [Audio podcast]. Retrieved from https://armchairexpertpod.com/pods
- Silvers, B., Stewart Holland, S. (Producers). The Nuanced Life [Audio podcast]. Retrieved from http://www.pantsuitpoliticsshow.com/blog-tnl

OTHER RESOURCES

- *The Great Hack*. Directed by Karim Amer, Jehane Noujaim, performance by Carole Cadwaddadr, David Carrol, Brittany Kaiser, 2019. *Netflix*. www.thegreathack.com
- Schwartz, Dr. Richard. (n.d.). The Internal Family Systems Model Outline. *IFS Institute*. Retrieved from https://ifs-institute.com/resources/articles/internal-family-systems-model-outline

BONUS LIBRARY INDEX
APPENDIX 2

You can find all of the bonus materials referenced in this book in the **Bonus Library** at: **www.wholeselflifestyle.com/working-parents/ bonus-library**.

ACKNOWLEDGMENTS

I was a teenager the first time I first realized I wanted to write a book. I've had dozens of book ideas in the decades since, but nothing ever felt right. Until now. This book wouldn't exist without the love, guidance, and endless support of a specific group of people.

Mom, you've been by my side in so many important moments of my life, and this is no exception. You cheered me on as I developed the idea for this book, plugged away at the first draft, and polished it until it was a true reflection of what was in my heart. You were the first person I trusted to read this book. Instead of focusing on criticism, you encouraged me to go deeper. You uncovered even more truth, insights and wisdom hidden inside me. This book is significantly better as a result. Thank you for being my guardian angel in so many ways.

To my sister, Emily: you were a seasoned parent long before I became a mom. You offered advice and perspective when I needed it most, but you always encouraged me to trust my instincts, too. You've talked me through my biggest challenges as a working parent. You've been there for me through thick and thin, and I can't imagine life without you. Thank you for holding a mirror up so I could explore my own personal journey of motherhood. I continue to learn so much from you. I am so grateful to have you in my life.

To my Pop Squad: Tracy, Kelly, Kim, Belinda, Anne, and

Emily. We left everything we knew when we moved to Austin, and y'all quickly became my Texas family. You bring a smile to my face every day, and it means the world to know you're all there to support me in my lowest moments too. Every working parent should be so lucky to have a crew like ours.

Michelle Mazur: I came to you with a jumble of random concepts and disconnected ideas. You masterfully helped me weave it all together until it made sense. The core of the Whole SELF Lifestyle began with you. You unlocked the conviction I feel about the message in this book and helped me refine my purpose in life. Thank you.

Many thanks to my wonderful editor, Karen Simmering, for your instant response times, your eagle eye, and for bringing this manuscript to life.

Ronald Cruz, thank you so much for designing this book cover. I came to you with a few ideas and some inspiration, and you created something beautiful.

To my podcast guests, who have enriched my knowledge in so many areas of life. Your insights have been invaluable, and your contribution to the world is inspiring. And to my devoted podcast listeners and The Argenal Institute community: you've been on this path of understanding the complexities of working parenthood with me for years now. I can't tell you how much I value the nuance and depth you've contributed to this process.

To my father, siblings, in-laws, and all of my other friends, colleagues, and strangers who have inspired my soul growth along the way. You've made an enormous impact on me, and I appreciate each and every one of you. I hold you all in my heart.

To my boys, Beckett and Weston: you've been my greatest teachers. You made me a mother, and I couldn't be more honored to share this journey in life with you. The purity of your love, the joy in your belly laughs, and the wonder in your eyes makes every day a profound adventure. I am so grateful for you both. Thank you for being my sons.

And finally, to my loving husband, Joey. I don't even know where to begin. This book will be published on the 10th anniversary of the day we met, and you've been by my side ever since. You've supported my wild ideas and my most ambitious dreams. Your commitment, empathy, and love as a husband, father and as a human motivates me to be the best version of myself I can be. Everything that's good in my life starts with you. Thank you for everything you do, and for everything you are.

ABOUT THE AUTHOR

Sarah Argenal, MA, CPC is on a mission to eradicate the burnout epidemic that's crushing working parents so they can finally enjoy these precious years of their lives. She is the founder of The Argenal Institute based in Austin, TX, host of the popular Working Parent Resource Podcast, and creator of the Whole SELF Lifestyle™ Method, a sustainable and long-term approach to personal fulfillment in the modern world.

Sarah combines twenty years of experience in areas such as psychotherapy, professional coaching, teaching, and complex project management to help working parents reclaim their time, energy, and identity. She has been featured in publications such as *NBC News, Healthline, Thrive Global, Working Mother*, and *PsychCentral*, and is a frequent guest on business and parenting podcasts around the world. Sarah lives with her husband and two sons in Austin, Texas. Visit **www. argenalinstitute.com** to learn more.

BEFORE YOU GO

Two final notes before you go.

First, would you mind leaving an honest rating and review on **Amazon**, **Goodreads**, or wherever you bought this book? Your comments would be extremely helpful to other overwhelmed working parents who are trying to decide whether this book might be valuable for them. I would really appreciate your thoughts.

Second, if you would like to stay in touch, receive free resources and tips, and learn more about the various ways I support busy working parents, please visit me at **www.argenalinstitute.com** to learn more, or email me at **hello@argenalinstitute.com** if you'd like to connect. I would love to hear from you!